MUSEUMS DISCOVERED

The Oskar Reinhart Collections

Edited by Leslie Shore

Editorial staff: Eve Sinaiko,
Alison de Lima Greene, Sandra Moy,
and Anthony Strianse

Translated by Margot Dembo
Color photography by Foto-Studio H. Humm

ISBN: 0-934516-41-3
Library of Congress Card Catalog Number: 81-50896

© 1981 by Woodbine Books, Inc., Fort Lauderdale, Florida
All rights reserved.
Printed in the United States of America.

Created for Woodbine Books, Inc., by
Shorewood Fine Art Books
475 Tenth Avenue
New York, N.Y. 10018

Thanks are due to Dr. Lisbeth Stähelin of
the Oskar Reinhart Collection for her
gracious assistance.

Plate 205, *Portrait of Mateu Fernández de Soto,*
by Pablo Picasso, reproduced courtesy of
S.P.A.D.E.M., Paris, and V.A.G.A., New York.

MUSEUMS DISCOVERED

The Oskar Reinhart Collections

by Franz Zelger

Woodbine Books
Ft. Lauderdale, Florida

Created by Shorewood Fine Art Books, New York

Introduction

Winterthur is a Swiss industrial and commercial town not far from Zurich. Its population is less than 100,000, but during the first half of this century it became an art center of international standing. This was due neither to the fame of any of its ecclesiastical or civic buildings, nor to its general appearance, but to the activities of a group of collectors which resulted in the establishment of several museums and collections whose contents are of a rare richness. The name most closely associated with Winterthur's importance as an art center is that of Oskar Reinhart (1885–1965), a great collector belonging to a highly regarded family of Winterthur merchants, whose patronage of the arts attracted attention far beyond the frontiers of the country. Thanks to his donations, the town now possesses two significant collections, the Oskar Reinhart Collection, housed in his former residence above the town, and the Oskar Reinhart Foundation, located in the center of the city.

His father, Theodor Reinhart, was himself an important patron of artists and cultural life: he was convinced that a small country like Switzerland could only fulfill its cultural obligations with intensive participation on the part of the private sector. He felt that it was his obligation "to make the works of artists available to the community by making donations and establishing foundations. These would become a means to further culture and would become the guiding force leading from materialism to the realm of idealistic spheres of interest." Thus, for his children, Theodor Reinhart was the example of a great Maecenas. Georg, his eldest son, became a well-known collector of European and Asian art. Another son, Hans, became a poet and devoted his energies to literature and the theater, while his brother Werner took a special interest in music and was closely associated with composers such as Stravinsky, Schönberg, Webern, Berg, Krenek, and many others.

He was also a patron of the poet Rainer Maria Rilke, whom he enabled to spend his last years at the Château Muzot in the Valais.

Oskar Reinhart, the youngest son, was born in Winterthur in 1885 and started to support the visual arts at an early age. Later in life, he would recall the atmosphere in his father's house and speak of his great good fortune in being able to grow up among artists and to learn from them how to use his eyes. His schoolboy writings clearly reveal that he was far more strongly attracted to art than to commerce as a way of life, but he bowed to his father's wishes and entered the family firm, in whose service he travelled first to Paris and London, and later to India. But wherever his work took him, he never failed to visit museums, private collections, and artists' studios, to buy books on the subject of art and to take an interest in auctions in that field. What impressed him most was the big exhibition of German nineteenth-century painters at Berlin in 1906, the "Exhibition of the Century." He received additional stimuli from an exhibition of modern French painting at Zurich in 1917, and from the books of the renowned art historian Julius Meier-Graefe, in particular his *Entwicklungsgeschichte der modernen Kunst*. Reinhart was also personally acquainted with Meier-Graefe.

Slowly but steadily he built up a collection. In 1924, when he was thirty-nine, he withdrew from the family business in order to devote himself entirely to art. That same year, he acquired the villa "Am Römerholz." There he finally able to realize his dream of building a gallery of his own, constructing it in the form of a large hall with a skylight roof, connected to the living apartments by means of a winter garden. In the years that followed, the collection was enriched so that it can now bear comparison with the finest museums in the world. It was later divided into two parts: the "Am Römerholz" Collection, which was private

Oskar Reinhart in 1948

until Reinhart's death, and has remained in his villa, and the Oskar Reinhart Foundation, which occupies a separate building and was a public gallery from the time of its inception. This latter contains works by Swiss, German, and Austrian artists, while the Collection has a great variety of masterpieces.

The Oskar Reinhart Foundation

As early as 1930, Oskar Reinhart, a bachelor without any direct heirs, informed the Winterthur Town Council that he wished to make part of his collection available to the public. This gesture was the product of an idea he had been nursing for a long time; for from the very beginning his activity as a collector had been marked by a high sense of social responsibility. He never lost sight of his obligation to place his knowledge and possessions at the service of the community, an attitude illustrated by the words he used in 1939, when opening an exhibition in Bern which included some of his pictures: "Although

works of art like these may be the legal property of an individual, in the higher sense they belong to the general public, and their owner is not entitled to regard himself as anything more than their custodian."

In the meantime, a search had begun in Winterthur for a suitable building to house these works of art. In the end, a disused school building was chosen. Known as the *Alte Gymnasium*, it was a large building erected between 1838 and 1842 on what was once the green belt that had surrounded the town. Its architectural design is typical of the period of most of the pictures it was to house. In compliance with the founder's wishes, the conversion of the building included construction of a number of replicas of salons in which the pictures could be displayed alongside furniture of their own period. As a result, the building acquired a special atmosphere, resembling that of a private home. This collection was named the Oskar Reinhart Foundation.

In 1951, the Foundation was opened to the public. The museum consisted of a self-contained group of works selected by the donor from his collection and comprising more than 500 pieces by Swiss, German, and Austrian artists of the eighteenth, nineteenth, and twentieth centuries. In subsequent years, it was expanded by the addition of other important pictures. Reinhart's "fondest wish to offer the enjoyment of good art to many recipients" was thus fulfilled. In the very year of the opening of the Foundation, the University of Zurich bestowed an honorary degree of Doctor of Philosophy upon "the knowledgeable connoisseur and exemplary collector of Western art." The same distinction already had been conferred upon him by the University of Basel in 1932.

The Foundation museum has a character of its own, mainly due to Reinhart's concept of collecting coupled with the formative influence of the 1906 Berlin "Exhibition of the Century." At that exhibition, its promoters—Hugo von Tschudi, Alfred Lichtwark, Julius Meier-Graefe—had aimed at a reevaluation of German artistic activity, and for that reason they excluded all kinds of academic art, historical pieces, and paintings with an anecdotal background. Instead, they concentrated their attention on little-known and forgotten works. Although it may be difficult today to believe it, the latter category included both the Romantics and the Realists. The organizers set about rediscovering the poetry, the feeling for nature, and the pictorial aspects of art: this example was taken up and pursued by Reinhart.

Of the many pictures included in the "Exhibition of the Century," he subsequently acquired more than twenty for his own collection.

If painters like Caspar David Friedrich, Philipp Otto Runge, Georg Friedrich Kersting, and Ferdinand Olivier were initially saved from oblivion in Berlin, Reinhart created the most important collection of German Romantics outside of Germany. Friedrich's *Chalk Cliffs, Rügen*, Runge's *Moonrise*, and Kersting's *Man Reading by Lamplight* belong among the most significant works created in Germany at that time.

Although Reinhart was a great collector of French art, his earliest commitment was to German painting. In 1913, he had acquired as one of his first pictures Max Liebermann's *Child with Apple*, and, in 1916, his *On the Way to School in Edam*. A little later, in a 1922 letter, he expressed the hope that he could bring together a carefully selected collection of German pictures. A copious but select survey of the work of the Romantic school was completed with a large number of works by the following generation of artists up to Karl Hofer. Included are pictures in the category of *The Artist's Mother* by Hans Thoma, *The Village Politicians* by Wilhelm Leibl, and *Iphigenia* by Anselm Feuerbach. Realism and idealism form a focal point for the collection. In addition to the Germans—Thoma, Leibl, Trübner, Feuerbach, and Marées—the Swiss—Albert Anker, Robert Zünd, Rudolf Koller, and Arnold Böcklin—are particularly represented by important works. Although Austrian painters are represented by relatively fewer works, such paintings as Waldmüller's *View of Arco* stand out equally because of their artistic worth. But Reinhart's choice of paintings—both German and Swiss—continually reveals that he used the criteria of French art and of Impressionism in particular, as had the organizers of the "Exhibition of the Century." In other words, he preferred intimate, "picturesque" paintings that display an affinity to nature. This taste often guided his interest toward a single aspect of an artist's oeuvre, such as his early works or his sketches: it was for this reason, for example, that he chose nothing but small works by Menzel from the first half of that artist's creative period. He chose to have Blechen represented by only a few landscape impressions full of light. And he preferred the earlier, painterly Leibl to the artist's later, more linear works, acquiring paintings like Leibl's *Portrait of Lina Kirchdorffer*, with its fine technique, which reminds one of Manet. This preference also guided his choice of

The Oskar Reinhart Foundation

works by Böcklin and Hodler. He acquired drafts, first impressions, poetic, refined, painterly pictures by Böcklin—those which, not coincidentally, Meier-Graefe, the author of the critical volume on Böcklin, *Der Fall Böcklin*, valued highly. At the same time, he avoided the more pathos-filled and luminous canvases of this artist. Similarly, Ferdinand Hodler's strongly symbolic figure compositions found no place in Reinhart's collection. Instead, the emphasis is on the realistic early work of this artist.

This emphasis enabled Reinhart to break new ground, particularly in the field of Swiss painting. In fact, he rescued a number of forgotten painters from oblivion, such as François Ferrière, Caspar Wolf, a pioneer of alpine painting, Friedrich Simon, Frédéric Dufaux, and Daniel Ihly.

All in all, in the words of Georg Schmidt, Reinhart sought "the bright rather than the gloomy; the simple rather than the complex; the tender rather than the harsh; the sensually pleasurable rather than the spiritually expressive."

This personal touch, a degree of congruity, and the consistently high quality of the works featured are what

The Romantics Room in the Foundation

give the Oskar Reinhart Foundation its specific character and balanced structure.

The Oskar Reinhart Collection "Am Römerholz"

The enthusiastic response aroused by the Foundation and by an exhibition in Winterthur of other works that had remained in Reinhart's private collection reinforced the collector's desire to ensure that the works of art in his possession would be handed down to posterity as a self-contained ensemble. When he died in 1965, he made it possible to implement this desire, for he left some 180 paintings, drawings, and sculptures—almost all of them masterpieces of the first rank—to the Swiss confederation,

together with his private villa, "Am Römerholz."

After his death, the villa was renovated to fulfill the requirements of a modern gallery, without, however, destroying the elegant and gracious effect of the building. Today, visitors will find a broad spectrum of choice works, some of them by Old Masters, and others by French painters and sculptors of the nineteenth century. From the miniature *Annunciation* by an Upper Rhenish master of the early fifteenth century to the *Portrait of Mateu F. de Soto* by Picasso, one masterpiece follows another. It is no coincidence that the Venetian colorists Jacopo Bassano and Jacopo Tintoretto are placed in the vestibule: they prepare us for a feast of color. These works draw the visitor into the Renaissance Room, where Pieter Bruegel's wintery and snowy *Adoration* hangs over the fireplace; it is flanked by Cranach's portraits of a self-confident bourgeois couple. Next to them hang works by Holbein and Gerard David, and Grünewald's drawing of a lamenting woman. A Louis XVI Salon, light-filled and carpeted in rush-green—a room apparently intended for chamber music—is the most beautiful setting imaginable for Watteau, Fragonard, Boucher, and Chardin. Then comes what was once the library, which has been converted into the graphics room. It alone is worth a visit to the collection—for here are found such works as Degas's pastel of a dancer and Cézanne's masterful watercolors. Towards the west there is a bright passageway, separated from the garden outside by a glass wall. This is the so-called winter garden, in which sculptures of the late nineteenth and early twentieth centuries (such as those by Rodin and Maillol) are exhibited. Another small room is devoted exclusively to the work of Daumier, an artist who especially interested Reinhart. In the large gallery, with its immense fireplace, Renaissance table, and Louis XIV armchairs, is the focal point of the collection: the French Masters of the nineteenth century. Here are the paintings of Jacques Louis David, Ingres, and Daumier; groups of works by Géricault, Delacroix, and Courbet; paintings by Toulouse-Lautrec and Van Gogh. Here also are works by those artists to whom French painting owes so much: Rubens and Constable. Corot and Renoir dominate the adjoining north room. Corot is represented by nine pictures, uncomplicated in subject, all of them Realist landscapes and figure studies. It is works of this genre that are the basis of Corot's importance—none of his once-celebrated mythological and historical scenes are in the collection. The opposite wall is reserved for Renoir, Reinhart's favorite painter. Painting is celebrated as a riot of color; in pictures such as *Confidences* and *La Grenouillère* it achieves its zenith. An entirely different world is revealed in the next room, which contains works of the Spanish and Dutch schools dating from the seventeenth to the early nineteenth century. El Greco's *Portrait of the Cardinal Inquisitor* stands out among a group of Goya paintings. The pale red of the Cardinal's robe is echoed by a strident scream of the bloody salmon slices in Goya's still life. And then, in the rear of the gallery, is the last high point: the paintings of Manet, Sisley, and Cézanne.

Thus, the Oskar Reinhart Collection is entirely unconventional in concept, for it is not built up in accordance

The Oskar Reinhart Collection "Am Römerholz"

with art-historical precepts, nor in accordance with chronological, didactic, or geographical associations. Instead, the emphasis is placed on problems of light and color. It would be difficult to name another private collection that makes the visitor so aware of the power of color as at Römerholz. Oskar Reinhart was attracted more to the painterly than to the graphic in art. There are only a few pictures in the collection that are distinctly and fundamentally linear in conception. Even these are works that are distinguished by a delicate coloring: the *Annunciation* by an Upper Rhenish master, Holbein's *Lady Widmerpole*, Cranach's portraits of Cuspinian and his wife. Reinhart's preferences become especially clear in his choices among the Impressionists. He selected twelve pictures by Renoir, two each by Sisley and Pissarro, and one by Monet. That type of Impressionism in which forms dissolve and vanish in light is disdained. Reinhart sought in the painterly—in the language of brush and color—an atmospheric density and clarity of expression. His aesthetic ideal was fulfilled in works that addressed an expert knowledge of art and at the same time appealed to the senses.

Reinhart also took immense pleasure in bringing together works of art whose affinity with one another transcends the boundaries of period and style. The Collection,

The Renaissance Room in the Collection

built up as it was by careful selection and a high sense of quality, thus impresses us as being itself a balanced composition, in which every element is related to the whole. The collection itself possesses something of the secret inner order of a masterpiece. A common essence joins works as different in content and epoch as Bruegel's proto-impressionistic winter landscape, Gerard David's *Pietà*, and paintings by Chardin, Corot, and the Impressionists. The luminous blue of Mme Ingres's shawl strikes an unexpected chord with the muted blue of Picasso's portrait of de Soto. We find a Constable alongside a Koninck, or a Rubens next to a Courbet. We find Corot and Renoir, Van Gogh and Toulouse-Lautrec matched one against another, one combination of pictures reflecting a tender, silent, dreamy world,

another highlighting human and social abandonment.

The unmistakable character of this collection is due to the thoroughness and perseverance with which Reinhart built it. In 1916 he envisioned it in part as a "*musée imaginaire*," and from the onset he consciously directed his attention to works that he felt spoke to him personally. He then had the patience and endurance to wait—sometimes for decades—until he could acquire them. For instance, he kept track of Manet's *Café* for thirty years before he could finally bring it into his collection. Böcklin's *Paolo and Francesca* was on his ideal list of works as early as 1921, but this important painting was not added to the collection until 1945. In 1923, Reinhart had written, "In the future I shall concentrate even more strictly upon those masters who are closest to me, rather than adhere to the museum principle of possessing a little of everything. My passion is for Daumier, Delacroix, Renoir, Courbet. I would particularly like to enlarge my collection with Daumier." In this he was extraordinarily successful, for he gathered together twenty paintings, watercolors, and drawings by Daumier. In addition, Reinhart assembled a major portion of Daumier's graphic work, in particular the newspaper caricatures that contributed so much to his fame. It is among these that we find the familiar law-court scenes and social satires that reflect the public life of the day, comprising a gigantic "*comédie humaine*." This high esteem for Daumier shows again that Reinhart was in sympathy with Meier-Graefe, who placed the paintings of Daumier at the side of those of Michelangelo and Rembrandt. The most recent works in the collection are a painting from the Blue Period of Picasso and three of his drawings from the year 1919, roughly the time when Reinhart began to collect.

Oskar Reinhart was not seeking experimental work or innovative art for his collection; instead, he was looking for fundamentally valid work from the past, work that built bridges to the future. In so doing, he trod unconventional paths at a time when pictures like those by the Impressionists and Post-Impressionists were far from receiving the same high esteem in which they are held today. The result is a collection which the great sculptor Maillol described as "the finest museum in the entire world." (Frère, Conversations de Maillol.)

Dr. Franz Zelger,
Director

Plate List

The Oskar Reinhart Foundation

JEAN ETIENNE LIOTARD

b. Geneva, 1702
d. Geneva, 1789

Turkish Lady with a Young Girl

Ca. 1738–42 or later
Pastel on parchment
69.5 x 54.5 cm. (27³/8 x 21⁷/16 in.)
Acquired 1935

The Reinhart Foundation is rich in paintings from French-speaking Switzerland, and particularly from Geneva. For example, Jean Etienne Liotard has a room to himself in the museum. Liotard, an important figure in portrait painting, had a distinguished clientele in Rome, Constantinople, Vienna, Paris, London, and elsewhere.

This picture shows a woman and a young girl in Turkish dress. The woman is wearing a turban, a striped jacket, a silk skirt decorated with flowers and, under it, silk pantaloons. In her left hand she is holding a long pipe. Her right hand is extended toward the girl as if she wishes to ask her to come closer. Both are wearing conspicuous pattens, but the lady's—a sign of her social rank—are markedly higher than those of the girl. The difference in rank is also indicated by the cloth slippers the lady is wearing, while the girl's feet are bare inside her clogs.

This genre scene was probably painted by Liotard during his stay in Constantinople (1738–42) or perhaps later, in remembrance thereof. He created several versions of this theme, which are only slightly different from one another.

17

CASPAR WOLF

b. Muri (Aargau), 1735
d. Heidelberg, 1783

The Staubbach Falls in Lauterbrunnental

1774
Oil on canvas
81.5 x 54 cm. (32$^{1}/_{16}$ x 21$^{1}/_{4}$ in.)
Acquired 1947

Caspar Wolf's pictures reflect the interest that people had begun to take in the alpine regions in the eighteenth century, an interest expressed in the form of mountaineering expeditions, scientific studies, and literary works. Previously, the Alps had been treated as terrifying, dangerous, and mysterious, frightening and threatening.

Among the first to participate in this change of attitude was the Bernese scholar and poet Albrecht von Haller, whose poem *Die Alpen* achieved widespread acclaim when it was published in 1729, being translated into more than thirty languages during his lifetime. Later, Jean Jacques Rousseau's publications on natural philosophy contributed to the growing enthusiasm for the mountains. Soon, the scientists and poets were followed on their expeditions and rambles by tourists, and the Swiss Alps became one of Europe's most popular places to visit. It was in this context that Caspar Wolf was commissioned by a publisher to paint about 200 mountain landscapes, which were intended for tourists and which in many cases were widely distributed in print or aquatint form. Wolf was in fact the pioneer of alpine painting, but he was at the same time an artist of considerable standing in Europe. He was one of the first to venture personally into the upper mountain regions in winter to paint the ice and snow. His works are thus of interest to geographers and glaciologists as well as to mountaineers and art historians.

Our picture shows the Staubbach Falls in Lauterbrunnental, one of the most famous sights of the Bernese Oberland. Ever since the eighteenth century, this waterfall has been a favorite subject of poets and painters, and it was visited by Goethe in 1779. Lord Byron mentions a visit to the Staubbach Falls in his diary for autumn 1816, and a verse of *Manfred* expresses his response to the experience. Wolf's painting is undoubtedly one of the most impressive of the visual representations of this subject, for he did not confine himself to expressing his delight in the falling water; he also noted the finest gradations of light and shade, and carefully studied the forms of the rock. His human figures, looking like insects, emphasize the majesty and might of the mountains and of the falls themselves.

19

HENRY FUSELI

b. Zurich, 1741
d. London, 1825

Nude Man Carrying a Clothed Woman on His Shoulder

1798–1800
Pencil on paper
37.8 x 28.5 cm. (14⁷/8 x 11¹/4 in.)

The Swiss-born Henry Fuseli, who settled in England, is one of the most universal figures in the world of European art and ideas of the eighteenth and nineteenth centuries. He depicted the works of Shakespeare and Milton in a series of pictures, and painted scenes from the poetry of Homer, Dante, and Wieland. In addition, he was a writer, poet, art theoretician, literary critic, and a professor at the Royal Academy.

The Reinhart Foundation owns an oil painting and several important drawings by this artist. This drawing is an unfinished sketch for the *Vision of the Flood*, of which only the second version has been preserved (Kunstmuseum, Winterthur). It is related to the cycle of forty-seven Fuseli paintings (1790–1800) based on the works of the English poet Milton. The "Milton Gallery," which was subsidized by the banker and historian William Roscoe, was not a great success when it opened to the public in 1799, although it brought the artist recognition and a few faithful patrons and well-wishers. In our drawing, a nude, frightened man, carrying a partially clothed woman on his shoulder, is fleeing up a cliff. The style of the drawing undeniably reveals Fuseli's admiration for Michelangelo.

21

WILHELM VON KOBELL

b. Mannheim, 1766
d. Munich, 1853

Group of Hunters
at the Tegernsee

1824
Oil on wood
40.5 x 52 cm. (15 $^{15}/_{16}$ x 20 $^{1}/_{2}$ in.)
Acquired 1948

In the first half of the nineteenth century, Wilhelm von Kobell ranked among the most important painters of battle scenes in Munich. In addition, he became well known for his precisely painted tableaux of doll-like figures on horseback, which he created for the local nobility and for the tradition-conscious citizenry. Our picture belongs among these works. It shows three elegantly dressed riders and one hunter in a sweeping landscape. The two riders in the foreground are engaged in conversation while the one in the rear seems to be giving directions to the hunter. In the background, one recognizes the Tegernsee Monastery, which has been the country seat of the royal house of Bavaria since 1817. In his presentation of the landscape, Kobell has adhered only partially to reality.

23

FIRMIN MASSOT

b. Geneva, 1766
d. Geneva, 1849

and

JACQUES LAURENT AGASSE

b. Geneva, 1767
d. London, 1849

Agasse with Bulldog

Ca. 1795
Oil on cardboard
35 x 30.7 cm. (13³/₄ x 12¹/₁₆ in.)
Acquired 1940

In a corner of a room, the painter Jacques Laurent Agasse is having a beer. He is seated in an unconventionally relaxed fashion next to a bulldog, and smiles thoughtfully at the onlooker. This portrait was created jointly by Massot and Agasse, most likely in 1795, when the two friends met in Lausanne. Massot, the portraitist of Geneva society and elegant promenade scenes, probably did the figure. Agasse, the painter of animals, probably painted the dog. The two artists had collaborated for some time before the creation of this Winterthur portrait.

25

JACQUES LAURENT AGASSE

b. Geneva, 1767
d. London, 1849

Landing Stage near Westminster Bridge

1818
Oil on canvas
35 x 53.5 cm. (13³/₄ x 21¹/₁₆ in.)
Acquired 1941

Agasse's *Landing Stage near Westminster Bridge* is particularly charming and though small in format produces a monumental effect. The picture reproduces a scene from the early days of the sport of rowing. The race it shows was initiated in 1715 by the actor Thomas Doggett for the Thames watermen, and has been repeated every year since then. At the time Agasse painted this picture, rowing clubs already existed in London. The red garment worn by the man on the left carrying an oar is probably an allusion to the orange-colored coat that Doggett awarded as a prize to the winner of his first race, thus originating the name the event still bears, "Doggett's Coat and Badge." The viewer stands below a massive arch of Westminster Bridge looking toward Waterloo Bridge, newly completed in 1817 and here bathed in bright sunshine. The view embraces Somerset House and various buildings on the left bank of the Thames. It was just at this period that John Constable began to concern himself with the same subject, but it was probably Canaletto who first discovered bridge arches as a subject, noting that they provided a picture with a "frame within a frame," as illustrated in his work *London Seen Through an Arch of Westminster Bridge* (Collection of the Duke of Northumberland). It was not long before this subject became commonplace in other countries too, and it persisted as a popular theme well into the nineteenth century.

A notable feature of the Agasse picture is the way the middle ground and background are painted, with the powerful contrasts in the clouded sky, producing an atmosphere almost anticipating the Impressionists. According to his personal catalogue, Agasse painted other Thames scenes viewed from Westminster Bridge which have nearly the same format as the Winterthur painting.

JACQUES LAURENT AGASSE

The Flower Seller

1822
Oil on canvas
35 x 43.5 cm. (13³/₄ x 17¹/₈ in.)
Acquired 1954

Jacques Laurent Agasse made his name in England as an animal painter. In 1800 he moved to London and was almost immediately included in Royal Academy exhibitions. Patricians, nobility, and the Royal Court were the sources of his commissions. He portrayed horses and hounds for their owners, painted in stables, parks, and paddocks, and produced pictures of giraffes, apes, leopards, lions, and gnus in the menageries and zoos which enjoyed a great popularity at that time. His pictures reveal the influence of George Morland and George Stubbs. Agasse also frequently painted animals as part of genres and other scenes. His *Flower Seller* presents a scene from everyday life in London and its mood and penetrating vision are reminiscent of the novels of Charles Dickens. The district shown is probably in the area of Newman Street, where the artist lived at that time, and the background is probably one of the squares of Soho, either Soho Square itself or Fitzroy Square. Hawkers and their barrows had already appeared in English paintings of the eighteenth century, for instance in Henry Walton's picture *The Cherry Barrow* (1779; private collection, England). In this case, the flower seller is probably a self-portrait of Agasse, while the children are most likely those of Agasse's landlord, Booth.

Agasse mentions two versions of *The Flower Seller* in his personal catalogue: "1822 . . . May. The flowers. cart . . . of the spring. 18. by 14″ [45.7 x 35.6 cm.] . . . 1826 . . . Copy of the picture of the flowers Cart. Small."

The sizes given allow one to assume that this entry concerns the Winterthur canvas, which thus must have been painted in 1822. The second version is currently in a private collection in Geneva.

29

JOSEPH ANTON KOCH

b. Obergiblen im Lechtal
   (Tyrol), 1768
d. Rome, 1839

The Wetterhorn

1824
Oil on canvas
91 x 81 cm. (35^{13}/$_{16}$ x 31^{7}/$_{8}$ in.)
Acquired 1950

Pictured here is the Wetterhorn in the Bernese Oberland, a region which is one of the most beloved tourist attractions in Switzerland. Koch, a native of the Tyrol, painted this monumental alpine scene not in connection with a trip to Switzerland, but rather in Rome in 1824. The artist had spent the years 1792 to 1794 in Switzerland, where, especially in the Bernese Oberland, he made numerous drawings and sketches upon which he drew later when he was working on paintings. This painting, however, is supposed to have been based on a print by an unknown young Swiss artist, presumably after an engraving or a colored etching. The flowers and plants in the left foreground were painted by Koch's friend Ludwig Richter, according to the latter's own statement.

31

CASPAR DAVID FRIEDRICH

b. Greifswald, 1774
d. Dresden, 1840

Town at Moonrise

Ca. 1817
Oil on canvas
45 x 32 cm. (17$^3/_4$ x 12$^5/_8$ in.)
Acquired 1931

One of the largest collections of paintings in the Oskar Reinhart Foundation is that of the German Romantics. Among these, the works by Caspar David Friedrich are worthy of particular attention. For this artist, landscape painting was the expression of a personal religious feeling. His pictures are often difficult to understand and cannot always be reliably interpreted. Night, moonlight, and twilight play an important part in the painting of the Romantics as well as in their literature and music. Friedrich's *Town at Moonrise* is full of symbolism. The town in the background is a complete invention based on his native Greifswald, and must be regarded as a vision of the Beyond, while the anchor is a symbol of hope and resurrection, and the full moon represents Christ. It is significant that the artist substituted Neo-Gothic ornaments for the actual Baroque ones on the Church of St. Nicholas at Greifswald, which can be recognized to the left of the moon, for the Gothic formal language bore a particular religious significance at that time.

33

CASPAR DAVID FRIEDRICH

Woman by the Sea

Ca. 1818
Oil on canvas
21.5 x 30 cm. (8$^1/_2$ x 11$^{13}/_{16}$ in.)
Acquired 1932

This picture belongs to a group of small seascapes which Friedrich painted after a sojourn at the Baltic Sea. In the left background, one recognizes the chalk cliffs of the coast of Rügen, and Cape Arkona located on the north of the island. The motif of the figure with its back turned assumes an important place in Friedrich's work. It symbolizes the isolation of man as well as his turning toward eternity. Thus, a solitary woman sits dreamily gazing over the open sea into the distance. She has seated herself upon a rock which can be interpreted in Friedrich's symbolic language as the image of Faith. "The white cliffs of the chalk mountains join with the white sails of the distant boats to represent another world, bright and distant. . . . The nets and the fishing boats . . . which move in the safety of the coastline, belong to this world, a world of trouble and toil." (Börsch-Supan and Jähnig, *Caspar David Friedrich*, no. 245.)

CASPAR DAVID FRIEDRICH

Chalk Cliffs, Rügen

1818
Oil on canvas
90 x 70 cm. (35⁷/16 x 27⁹/16 in.)
Acquired 1930

Chalk Cliffs, Rügen is not merely one of Friedrich's principal works but is indeed one of the best-known pictures produced by a German nineteenth-century painter. It was painted around 1818 as a souvenir of the artist's honeymoon and has since given rise to numerous attempts at interpretation. For example, there are differences of opinion about the topography and the figures seen from the back, ensconced in natural surroundings. The woman in the picture is probably Friedrich's wife, while the male figures could be a double self-portrait representing the artist viewing the foreground and background respectively. When looking at this picture and the way it shows distances and depths, one is reminded of the words of the painter's contemporary, the German philosopher Friedrich Schleiermacher: "To observe the Universe is the highest and most general formulation of religion." The sailboats, symbolizing souls setting out for the Beyond, bring to mind a line by Ernst Moritz Arndt: *"Flügel der Seele—schwellende Segel* (Wings of the Soul, billowing like sails)."

37

CASPAR DAVID FRIEDRICH

Riesengebirge Landscape

1828–30
Pen, brush, ink, watercolor,
    and pencil
24.6 x 33.8 cm. (9 11/16 x 13 5/16 in.)
Acquired 1935

In 1810, Caspar David Friedrich and Georg Friedrich Kersting wandered through the Riesengebirge, the highest part of the Sudetenland near the Czech-Schleswig border. This watercolor in the Reinhart Foundation is based upon studies Friedrich made during that time. The artist used the village of Warmbrunn as his base. Pictured here is the view across the Giersdorfer lakes toward the "Little Sturmhaube." It is characteristic of Friedrich's watercolors that this work shows a strong structural, tectonic element, while color plays a secondary role. Despite this, the soft interplay of yellow and grey is enchanting.

39

PHILIPP OTTO RUNGE

b. Wolgast (Pomerania), 1777
d. Hamburg, 1810

Evening

1802–03
Pen and ink on paper
72.5 x 51.8 cm. (28^9/$_{16}$ x 20^3/$_8$ in.)

Probably the most creative figure among the German Romantics was Philipp Otto Runge, who died at the early age of thirty-three. He was painter, draftsman, philosopher, poet, and color theorist in one. Toward the end of 1802, he began making sketches for a set of mural paintings to be entitled *Times of the Day*, symbolizing the Rule of God. *Morning, Midday, Evening,* and *Night* represent Becoming, Unfolding, Passing Away, and Trust in God.

Our drawing shows a sketch for *Evening*: at the bottom a lily sinks down into clouds. Roses climb up each side, and poppies, symbols of sleep, spread out from the center. A large figure in billowing robes floats at the top. Above the design appears the moon; farther down is a star. The plants are inhabited by children, sleeping, making music, and embracing.

40

41

PHILIPP OTTO RUNGE

Moonrise

1808
Oil on canvas on painted wood
93.5 x 202.5 cm. ($36^{13}/_{16}$ x $79^{3}/_{4}$ in.)
Acquired 1931

Runge painted *Moonrise* for his friend Friedrich Perthes, a Hamburg bookseller and publisher. The painting was intended for an alcove above a sofa.

Perthes was in close contact with contemporary writers, poets, and scholars of his time (Görres, Arndt, the Schlegel brothers, Savigny), some of whom he recruited for his publishing house. His wife was the daughter of the poet Matthias Claudius.

Runge aimed at a symbolical, naturally religious style of painting, expressive of his own feelings of mystical piety. The decorative alcove piece, with its charming colors, shows the figures of two boys, one awake and the other sleeping and each with a poppy, before a rising moon. They symbolize the transition from eventide to darkness and the renewal of light.

43

FERDINAND OLIVIER

b. Dessau, 1785
d. Munich, 1841

St. Peter's Cemetery in Salzburg

Ca. 1816
Pencil on paper
24 x 34 cm. (9$^{1}/_{2}$ x 13$^{3}/_{8}$ in.)
Acquired 1936

The Austrian city of Salzburg exerted a strong fascination on the Romantic artists, especially on Ferdinand Olivier, who was connected with the Catholic brotherhood of German artists called the "Nazarenes." St. Peter's Cemetery, which dates back to Roman times and which is the most ancient Christian burial site in the city, offered him a profound experience. Olivier captured this cemetery, which is still well known today, in several versions, one of which is in the Reinhart Foundation. In this precise drawing, he emphasized the hidden nooks, the secluded corners of the grounds, and the intermingling of diverse styles and architectural periods. And yet the thought of mortality does not inspire melancholy or pain here. For the Romantic, a cemetery is not only a *memento mori* but also the place which connects him with his ancestors and thus with History.

45

GEORG FRIEDRICH KERSTING

b. Güstrow, 1785
d. Meissen, 1847

Man Reading by Lamplight

1814
Oil on canvas
47.5 x 37 cm. (18^{11}/$_{16}$ x 14^{9}/$_{16}$ in.)
Acquired 1948

Georg Friedrich Kersting, an important representative of German Romanticism, was a close friend of Caspar David Friedrich and was assisted by Goethe, who wrote of him in the fifteenth book of *Poetry and Truth*, recommended him to the Duke of Weimar, and organized a picture lottery for him.

This picture shows a man reading by candlelight in a high-ceilinged, simply furnished room. The wall is without decoration, and the furniture shows a combination of office-like simplicity and comfortable elegance. Caskets and boxes on shelves to the right suggest that he is a collector or a scholar. The writing utensils and sealed letters also presumably indicate this. What at first seems to be a book may be a document file. A bell-pull suggests that a clerk might be within call. On the bare green wall over the man's head appear secretive shadows of which he, however, takes no note. He is totally absorbed in his work.

Kersting is a master at producing interiors charged with atmosphere, in which a person is integrated into the scene so as to form a harmonious entity.

47

FERDINAND GEORG WALDMÜLLER

b. Vienna, 1793
d. Hinterbrühl near Baden, 1865

View of Arco

1841
Oil on canvas
44.5 x 57.5 cm. (17$\frac{1}{2}$ x 22$\frac{5}{8}$ in.)
Acquired 1930

Waldmüller, together with Jakob and Rudolf Alt, represents midcentury Austrian painting at Winterthur. Their works are kept in a Biedermeier room, enchanting in its discreet elegance. Landscapes comprise a large portion of Waldmüller's work, as well as realistic pictures, which mirror the world of the court and the bourgeoisie at the time of Metternich. Doubtless one of his most important works is *View of Arco*, a picture that he painted during a trip to Italy. Arco lies to the north of Lake Garda. This painting is distinguished by the breadth of its space, achieved through the interaction among fore-, middle-, and backgrounds—an innovation in the work of the artist. Especially impressive is the way in which Waldmüller combines an exact rendition of landscape with bright, clear sunlight, causing the strong colors to glow.

49

FRANZ KRÜGER

b. Grossbadegast, near Dessau, 1797
d. Berlin, 1857

Prussian Cavalry Outpost
in the Snow

1821
Oil on canvas
55 x 61.5 cm. (21⅝ x 24¼ in.)
Acquired 1932

Franz Krüger is well known for parade and military pictures. Here he paints, with absolute fidelity to reality, a scene which may be viewed in connection with the Napoleonic Wars. The snow-covered corpse of a fallen soldier (at the lower left corner) is discovered by a troop of horsemen. A shivering greyhound stands nearby. Krüger has brilliantly captured the ice-cold, bleak, stormy winter day, as well as the eerie, threatening mood, seen in the lighting and in the tense faces of the two riders in the foreground.

51

CARL BLECHEN

b. Cottbus, 1798
d. Berlin, 1840

The Construction
of the Devil's Bridge

1829
Oil on paper mounted on wood
15 x 22.5 cm. (5$^7/_8$ x 8$^7/_8$ in.)
Acquired 1932

It was characteristic of Oskar Reinhart that he acquired a series of oil sketches by Carl Blechen, an early exponent of outdoor painting. When Blechen was returning to Germany from Italy in October 1829, he sketched the legendary Devil's Bridge on the north side of the St. Gotthard Pass. Subsequently, he made two oil sketches and a large painting, which now hangs in the Neue Pinakothek in Munich; our painting is one of the small sketches. The Devil's Bridge is a scene that had fascinated artists ever since the eighteenth century. In addition to Blechen, the Englishman J.M.W. Turner also painted it most impressively. Blechen's picture shows the construction of the second bridge, completed in 1830. In front of it we recognize the old bridge—according to legend built by the Devil himself—which collapsed in 1888.

A ray of light lifts the two structures from the gloom of the surrounding mountain gorge and they shine forth as the spectacular focus of a dramatic landscape.

LOUIS LEOPOLD ROBERT

b. Les Eplatures (Neuchâtel), 1798
d. Venice, 1835

Girl from Procida

1822
Oil on canvas
81 x 68.5 cm. (31^7/$_8$ x 27 in.)
Acquired 1949

Louis Léopold Robert, a pupil of Jacques Louis David, was one of the greatest Swiss artists of the early nineteenth century. His painting has both classical and Romantic features. The *Girl from Procida* is one of several idealized pictures he produced of Italian women and girls. The proud beauty stands against a southern landscape, a sharply defined half-figure. Her face, framed by dark hair and painted in an enamel-like style, is turned toward the viewer. She wears a colorful costume trimmed with gold lace. As in Renaissance portraits, figure and landscape are carefully matched to one another. The girl might be described as the "Mona Lisa" of the Romantic period.

The picture is probably the one mentioned in earlier literature as the *Portrait of a Young Woman/Girl from Procida* that the Prussian king Friedrich Wilhelm III acquired in 1822 on the occasion of an exhibition organized in his honor in Rome.

55

LUDWIG RICHTER

b. Dresden, 1803
d. Dresden, 1884

The Shepherd and His Girl

1865
Pencil with color on paper
12.7 x 22 cm. (5 x 8 $^{11}/_{16}$ in.)

Like Moritz von Schwind, Ludwig Richter was a late Romantic. He became well known for his evocative landscapes, genre scenes, and especially for the woodcut illustrations he did for legends and fairy tales. He frequently made variations on his themes, so that there are several slightly differing versions of his drawing *Shepherd and His Girl*. In this one we see two rural lovers sitting on a hill. The girl is making a wreath out of branches. Nearby, the sheep of the shepherd are grazing—a soft poetic idyll.

MORITZ VON SCHWIND

b. Vienna, 1804
d. Niederpöcking/Starnbergersee, 1871

The Angels Appear to Genoveva

After 1833
Oil on wood
19.5 x 44 cm. (7^{11}/$_{16}$ x 17^3/$_8$ in.)
Acquired 1932

This long, narrow painting is a duplication by Schwind of a ceiling painting he had executed in 1833–34 for the Munich royal court building, which was destroyed in the Second World War. Schwind, who in his youth was a friend of the composer Franz Schubert and the poet Franz Grillparzer, brought great poetic imagination to numerous studies based on fairy tales, fables, and legends. His portrayal of the Genoveva cycle was inspired by Ludwig Tieck's drama *Leben und Tod der heiligen Genoveva* (*Life and Death of the Blessed Genoveva*). Genoveva, the daughter of the Duke of Brabant, was wrongfully accused of adultery and sentenced to death. She was able to escape to the Ardennes Forest. There she stayed with her son for six years, living on herbs and the milk of a doe, until her husband Siegfried accepted her innocence, found her again while hunting, and led her back to his castle. Schwind's picture shows Genoveva and two angels warding off menacing death with a crucifix. At the left we see Genoveva's son with the doe. The wide format which Schwind preferred is especially well suited to story-telling material. The old Genoveva legend, which was also set to music by Robert Schumann, was a theme which the nature-loving late Romantics found particularly attractive.

FRIEDRICH WASMANN

b. Hamburg ,1805
d. Merano, 1886

Girl with Curls

Ca. 1844
Pencil on paper
21.5 x 16.7 cm. (8^{1}/$_{2}$ x 6^{1}/$_{2}$ in.)

Friedrich Wasmann, who was born in Hamburg, is nowhere so generously represented outside his native land as at Winterthur. Portraits and nature studies from the south Tyrol and from Rome give an overview of the most fruitful creative period of this rather solitary artist. This drawing, *Girl with Curls*, has special charm: the transition from Romanticism to early Realism is clearly visible in the soft, dreamy facial contours and expression, as compared to the artist's exact observation and precise lines.

CARL SPITZWEG

b. Munich, 1808
d. Munich, 1885

The Painter in the Garden

1860–63
Oil on cardboard
21.5 x 34 cm. (8$\frac{1}{2}$ x 13$\frac{3}{8}$ in.)
Acquired 1947

Among the late Romantics, special mention should be made of Spitzweg, whose mostly small works provide a benevolent view of simple individuals, at the same time emphasizing their isolation and a certain innocence. Spitzweg frequently explored the theme of the painter in the landscape. Here, the seated artist, seen from the back in a sunny garden, is probably Spitzweg's friend, the painter Eduard Schleich (1812–74). The two painters went on several study trips together. Spitzweg's preference for idyllic atmosphere is illustrated by the peaceful attitude of the seated figure and by the garden overflowing with shrubs, grass, and flowers. A great deal of attention has been given to the sunlight, which suffuses the plants and illuminates the blossoms.

ALEXANDRE CALAME

b. Vevey, 1810
d. Menton, 1864

View of Geneva

Ca. 1855
Oil on cardboard
32 x 40 cm. (12⅝ x 15¾ in.)
Acquired 1933

Alexandre Calame, who lived in Geneva, became well known as a painter of mountains and enjoyed triumphant successes in the 1840s and 1850s. In Paris he was awarded honors; numerous students from various countries gathered about him; enthusiastic alpine tourists—Russian, German, and English—bought his paintings as souvenirs. While his large, crystal-clear studio paintings often seem academic, the small studies he painted from nature are marked by the freshness and spontaneity of direct experience. *View of Geneva* is an example of this. The silhouette of the city, produced with a few brushstrokes, appears in front of the mountainous backdrop formed by the Savoy Range. The study is reminiscent of certain pictures by Corot, whose representation of a similar subject and management of light and color particularly impressed Calame at the time. In 1855, Calame wrote: "Corot lies closest to my heart because of his ideas and his peaceful, gentle expression." (Guillaume, *Avant l'impressionisme en Suisse*.)

65

CHRISTIAN KØBKE

b. Copenhagen, 1810
d. Copenhagen, 1848

*View from Dosseringen
toward Østerbro*

1838
Oil on canvas
39.5 x 50.5 cm. (15⁹/₁₆ x 19⁷/₈ in.)
Acquired 1960

In the Reinhart Foundation an artist's significance is documented now and then through a single picture. This applies, for example, to Christian Købke, who died young and left only a small oeuvre, the quality of which, however, is attested to by *View from Dosseringen*. Reinhart, moreover, had to wait twelve years before he could buy a landscape by this artist. Only the good reputation of the Foundation moved the Copenhagen Museum to allow the collector to obtain at auction a painting which they would very much have liked to see in a public Danish collection.

At Winterthur it now bears witness to the quality of Danish art, existing here on a par with the early Realism of artists from Berlin, Munich, Vienna, and Geneva.

Købke frequently painted in Dosseringen, a garden-suburb of Copenhagen. In this painting, he painted the evening return of a sailboat on a sunny spring day in May. Two men are busy unrigging the boat, while three women talk on the dock. The sky is suffused with the softly bright light that Købke liked so much. The clouds, tinged lilac by the setting sun, are mirrored on the water's surface.

ADOLF VON MENZEL

b. Breslau, 1815
d. Berlin, 1905

Berlin Backyards in the Snow

1847–48
Oil on paper mounted on cardboard
13 x 24 cm. (5¹/₈ x 9¹/₂ in.)
Acquired 1938

Adolph von Menzel became known for his stately scenes from the life of Frederick the Great of Prussia, as well as for the portrayal of events at the court of Kaiser Wilhelm I. He also painted with subtle insight the people and simple themes of his own immediate surroundings. A large role is played in this connection by his "window pictures"—views from his Berlin apartment of streets, construction sites, and gardens. The present example is especially charming. It presents the view from Menzel's apartment on the Ritterstrasse of the backs of the houses across the way on a winter day. The artist was adept at capturing the mood and atmosphere of a place and season.

68

69

ADOLF VON MENZEL

Portrait of Mrs. Maercker

1848
Oil on canvas
37.5 x 28 cm. (14³/₄ x 11 in.)
Acquired 1948

This portrait, set in a middle-class interior, shows Mrs. Maercker, wife of C. A. Maercker, who was named Prussian Minister of Justice in 1848. A warm friendship existed between Menzel and the Maercker family. This small, full-length portrait charms one with its graceful portrayal and fine coloring.

ADOLF VON MENZEL

View from a Window

1867
Gouache on paper
29 x 22.5 cm. ($11^7/_{16}$ x $8^7/_8$ in.)

The exceptional charm of this small, unspectacular window-view lies in the way in which the artist leads the eye of the viewer from a plain interior out into the rich green of nature, the way he paints light passing through the curtains, and, above all, the way in which he captures the atmosphere of a fleeting moment. It is as if a breeze could move the open casements at any moment; as if the titmouse, peering curiously into the apartment, could fly off in the next instant; or the shade might unexpectedly roll down in front of the window and close off the view.

73

ARNOLD BÖCKLIN

b. Basel, 1827
d. San Domenico near Fiesole, 1901

Pan Among the Reeds

1856–57
Oil on canvas
138 x 99.5 cm. (54⁵/₁₆ x 39³/₁₆ in.)
Acquired 1928

The Swiss painter Arnold Böcklin was one of the main proponents of German idealist painting. Like Feuerbach, he spent a considerable portion of his life in Italy. He expressed his poetic imagination in clear, comprehensible forms and with a broad palette of color. The principal mythological figures in Böcklin's works are Pan, fauns, nymphs, tritons, and nereids. With *Pan Among the Reeds*, Böcklin takes up a theme which occupied him to the end of his creative life: the personification of the mood of a region using figures from ancient mythology who, for him, expressed that mood. This is his first version of *Pan*, completed in 1857, at the end of his first Roman sojourn. The second version was acquired by the Bavarian Court in 1859 for the Neue Pinakothek in Munich. With this, Böcklin earned public esteem for the first time.

In this first version of *Pan Among the Reeds*, the wood-god is partly concealed from the viewer's gaze, both formally and by the use of color, in the manner of the popular puzzle pictures of the time. The Munich picture seems more naturalistic: Pan is larger and more three-dimensional; the reeds are drawn more precisely and are clearly separated into three groups.

75

ARNOLD BÖCKLIN

Children Whittling May-Flutes

1865
Oil on canvas
64.5 x 96.5 cm. (25³⁄₈ x 38 in.)
Acquired 1927

This painting attests to Böcklin's love of children and music. It shows Böcklin at his most amiable, and both artistically and personally it belongs among his most joyful works. Here he painted, in rich detail and free of mythological references, a spring meadow, which like a peninsula extends into the water from left to right.

Two little naked musicians convey the atmosphere of the place. Böcklin was probably inspired to paint this scene by Ludwig Richter's woodcut *Kinderlust* (*Childish Joy*). The father of fourteen children, eight of whom died very young, Böcklin had a particularly close relationship to young people: "The more children I have, the more desire I have to work." Perhaps the most impressive description of his relationship with children appears in Angela Böcklin's *Memoirs*: "The characteristics of his personality were revealed most strikingly in his association with the children. . . . A great passionate love was evident, especially while the children were still small. He handled each one differently—each according to his individual character—for quite early on he also differentiated between them in his own preferences."

Böcklin created many caricatures for children, especially for his own. Some of them were based on James Fenimore Cooper's *Leatherstocking*, others were illustrations for fairy tales and pedagogical or moralistic drawings of people and animals. Therefore, it is in no way surprising that children assume an important place in Böcklin's work.

77

ARNOLD BÖCKLIN

Triton and Nereid

1877
Tempera on paper mounted
  on wood
44.5 x 65.5 cm. (17^{1}/$_{2}$ x 25^{13}/$_{16}$ in.)
Acquired 1929

Böcklin's numerous seascapes are inhabited by tritons and ne-reids. A nereid, one of the fifty daughters of the hoary sea god Nereus, is shown here, together with Triton, the son and servant of Poseidon.

In this color sketch, the artist portrays a nereid sprawling on a slippery rock in a lurid light. She is caressing a fantastic sea serpent. Triton, rising from the sea, seems to be uttering muffled cries. The figures are brought into complete harmony with nature in this painting.

The Winterthur picture is a preparatory work for a third, un-completed version of the same theme. Since two variations of this subject already existed, Böcklin's study was turned down by the acquisi-tion committee of the Berlin Nationalgalerie. Thereupon, the sculptor Reinhold Begas obtained it for himself.

ARNOLD BÖCKLIN

Paolo and Francesca

1893
Tempera and oil on canvas
110.5 x 80 cm. (43½ x 31½ in.)
Acquired 1949

Böcklin's painting depicts a scene from Dante's *Inferno*, fifth canto, verses 73ff.

In 1275, Francesca da Rimini was married to Gianciotto Malatesta for political reasons. In 1284, Malatesta murdered his wife and his brother, who had been having a love affair. This picture shows the unhappy, adulterous pair in Hell, floating free in a pale, eerie light against a dark background. The two floating figures remind one of the Pompeiian frescoes that had deeply impressed the artist. Francesca is turning away from her beloved in despair and anguish; Paolo, moved by passion, tries to draw her to him.

There is another portrayal of this motif in Böcklin's earlier *Lamentation* (1876; Nationalgalerie, Berlin), in which the Magdalen turns away from St. John in a gesture of solitary grief, and John grasps her rejecting left hand with both of his in an expression of comfort.

FRANK BUCHSER

b. Feldbrunnen (Solothurn), 1828
d. Feldbrunnen, 1890

Woodstock, Virginia

1867
Oil on canvas
24 x 33 cm. (9$^7/_{16}$ x 13 in.)
Acquired 1927

The Swiss painter Frank Buchser spent much of his life in foreign countries. From 1866 to 1871 he was in the United States of America. At the beginning of August 1867, the artist and his love of the time, Phryne, moved from the Allegheny Mountains of Grant County in West Virginia to Woodstock in the Shenandoah Valley, to draw studies of blacks. The beautiful, fertile landscape had been ravaged by the Civil War and the population had been reduced to poverty. The whites of the area suspected that the painter—with his studies of ragged blacks—wanted to draw attention to their exploitation in Virginia. Consequently, the pictures he had planned to do in Woodstock never materialized. But this sketch of the village street, painted with impetuous brushstrokes, and dated August 21, testifies to Buchser's stay there. The sketch is full of impressionistic details of daily life. Artistically, it belongs among the most outstanding works of his American stay and is an example of the high quality of the artist's improvised small-format oil sketches.

Woodstock 21 Aug 63.

ANSELM FEUERBACH

b. Speyer, 1829
d. Venice, 1880

Iphigenia II

1870
Oil on canvas
62.5 x 49.5 cm. (24⅝ x 19½ in.)
Acquired 1953

The objectives pursued by Anselm Feuerbach, the well-educated, sensitive son of an archaeologist, are quite different from those of the Realists Thoma and Leibl. Feuerbach's aim was to revive antiquity and, inspired by this desire, he painted *Iphigenia*, a work that occupies a central position in his oeuvre. This study of a head was made in preparation for the second version of the subject (Staatsgalerie, Stuttgart); he used as his model Lucia Brunacci, his Roman mistress at the time. She is seen in profile, her head half in shadow, leaning on her left hand, staring dreamily into the distance: "Her soul yearning toward the land of the Greeks," as Goethe put it.

Themes of protest against one's fate and the longing for one's native land had already been expressed in Euripides' tragedy *Iphigenia*. But it was Goethe who first raised these themes to symbolic significance for the nineteenth century: as the yearning of modern man for antique Greece.

83

ALBERT ANKER

b. Ins (Bern), 1831
d. Ins, 1910

The Artist's Young
Daughter Louise

1874
Oil on canvas
80.5 x 65 cm. (31^{11}/$_{16}$ x 25^9/$_{16}$ in.)
Acquired 1929

Albert Anker was among the most popular painters in Switzerland. His themes embraced the everyday life of the Bernese village of Ins where he lived. Moreover, he had an extraordinary sympathy for children. His fame, however, comes not only from the themes he painted, but also from his delicate style, which was influenced by the French masters.

A high point in children's portraiture is surely Anker's picture of his nine-year-old daughter Louise, who appears in this half-length portrait before a light-grey background. The girl is dressed up in the style of the 1860s. The yellowish jacket, the blue-and-white plaid skirt, the pendant she wears around her neck, all are decidedly elegant; but these accessories do not diminish her childish charm. From the way she holds her head, shoulder, and arm there emerges a youthful freshness and sauciness.

ALBERT ANKER

The Day Nursery

1890
Oil on canvas
79.5 x 142 cm. (31^5/$_{16}$ x 55^{15}/$_{16}$ in.)
Acquired 1950

This picture shows a scene from the daily routine of a nursery. The little ones are eating under the care of a nurse. Twelve children, ranging in age from about three to six years, sit around a simple table; another is off by himself near the door, drinking his soup. Anker places the nurse in the immediate foreground, so that she seems overly large next to the flock of children entrusted to her. Her serious, calm face radiates motherly solicitude, which is emphasized by her forward-leaning position. The children are represented less as a group than as individual personalities. The artist stresses the already distinct individual facial characteristics of the boys and girls; he observes every detail and incorporates it into the composition.

HANS THOMA

b. Bernau (Schwarzwald), 1839
d. Karlsruhe, 1924

The Artist's Mother in Her Room

1871
Oil on canvas
105 x 77.5 cm. (41³/₈ x 30¹/₂ in.)
Acquired 1927

Reinhart's great liking for Hans Thoma is at first sight surprising for a collector of nineteenth-century French art, but here again he only selected works that fitted into his program, pictures whose Realism relates to that of Courbet rather than being allegorical or anecdotal. One such picture is Thoma's portrait of his mother, in which he combines an almost tangible filial love with a sober objectivity of reproduction, to produce a work of art that goes far beyond being a portrait of an individual or a genre scene to become a general symbol of old age. It shows the living quarters the woman occupies, which, albeit small, are peaceful. She sits in the warm sunshine, absorbed in her Bible. Through the open window, next to the roof of the opposite house, a tiny triangle of sky can be seen.

"In the summer of 1871 I returned to Säckingen. There I painted my mother while she was reading in the sunlit attic chamber," reports the artist, in *Im Winter des Lebens*, about the origin of the painting. Thoma painted his mother frequently. Their close relationship throughout her life was based on a mutual affection. When he was seventy years old he wrote: "I was still her boy long after I had a grey beard, and she surrounded me with her total motherly care." (Thoma, *Im Herbst des Lebens*.)

89

HANS THOMA

Sorrento

1881
Oil on canvas
77 x 105 cm. (30⁵/₁₆ x 41³/₈ in.)
Acquired 1929

Thoma was commissioned by his patron Charles Minoprio of Liverpool to paint about ten different Italian landscapes. This view of Sorrento, with cloud-enveloped Monte Sant'Angelo a Tre Pizzi in the background, came into being in this connection. The picture is notable for its strong coloring. What especially impressed Thoma was the interaction of land and sea. In 1909, he wrote about this in his *Herbst des Lebens* (*Autumn of Life*): "The sea is unbelievably blue, and with a singular olive-green there develops a color harmony of the most beautiful sort; one would like to conclude from this that the olive tree and the sea belong together."

91

WILHELM LEIBL

b. Cologne, 1844
d. Würzburg, 1900

The Village Politicians

1877
Oil on canvas
76 x 97 cm. (29^{15}/$_{16}$ x 38^{3}/$_{16}$ in.)
Acquired 1953

Courbet's Realism forms the basis for Wilhelm Leibl's art, as is shown in this painting of 1877. Leibl aimed to portray peasant farmers in their parlors as accurately as possible, and he was certainly successful in doing so. Here, five men have gathered in the corner of a room, some of them self-confident, others distrustful, and still others fearful and tongue-tied, but all of them ruggedly individual. They are listening eagerly to one of their number (who might be the schoolmaster) as he reads from a document. This picture marks the transition in Leibl's development from a gentle style to a harder one with a tendency to linearity. All the details are precisely observed— the unshaven chins, the wrinkles, the dirty fingernails, the old, thread-bare clothes, the seam of a smock, the grain of the timber benches and the much-trodden floor. It is a typical feature of German paintings of the 1870s to place the figures prominently in the foreground.

MAX LIEBERMANN

b. Berlin, 1847
d. Berlin, 1935

On the Way to School in Edam

1904
Oil on canvas
69 x 82.5 cm. (27³/₁₆ x 32¹/₂ in.)
Acquired 1916

Liebermann's art developed from naturalistic beginnings to a specifically German Impressionism, whose main interpreter he became. *On the Way to School in Edam* was painted during an extended stay in the Dutch town. Liebermann made three versions, all of which have the same subject: children—dressed more or less identically as though they were in uniforms—walking to school through a sunny square.

Thematically, this canvas echoes the Dutch village street scenes which Liebermann had painted earlier and his *On the Way to School in Laren* (1898–99; Folkwang Museum, Essen) in particular. This picture of Edam, in its painterly conception, belongs among the most modern in the gallery.

95

FERDINAND HODLER

b. Bern, 1853
d. Geneva, 1918

Mademoiselle Lardet

1878
Oil on canvas
72 x 58.5 cm. (28³/8 x 23 in.)
Acquired 1940

One of the high points of the Reinhart Foundation collection is a group of more than thirty pictures by the Swiss painter Ferdinand Hodler—a selection that clearly shows the collector's preferences, for the emphasis is on the artist's early Realist period, while his later symbolic figure compositions have been omitted.

Hodler painted this portrait during his sojourn in Spain in 1878 and 1879. According to a letter he wrote to his friend Odier, it was painted in November 1878. Shown is the daughter of Charles Edouard Lardet, the Swiss Consul-General in Madrid.

Seen at three-quarter length, the girl, about seven years old, stands before a prussian-blue background. Her head is tilted a little to the side; large, deep-blue eyes under shapely, curved eyebrows gaze at the viewer. Her mouth is slightly ajar and accentuated on each side by a dimple. The left arm hangs down close to her side, the right hand is resting on a chair upholstered in cobalt blue, trimmed with ochre stripes. She wears a coatdress buttoned down the front, with lace-trimmed cuffs and collar. The gradation of the different blue tones in harmony with ochre, yellow, brown, and white is enchanting—a color combination preferred by Hodler. The relaxed brushwork in this portrait is visible in the sketchy treatment of the coat-dress and is especially clear in the hands. In addition to color, light also performs an important function; it falls in this painting from the upper right upon the girl, so that she is partially in the shade. Although the portrait of Lardet's daughter is not among the artist's frequently reproduced pictures, the intense coloring makes it a jewel of Hodler's early work.

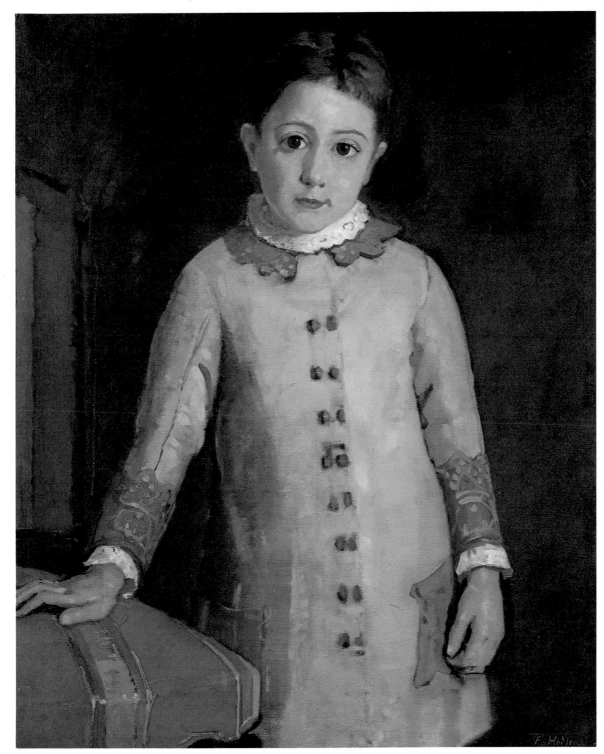

97

FERDINAND HODLER

***Self-Portrait in a
Stand-Up Collar***

1879
Oil on canvas
72 x 52 cm. (28³/₈ x 20¹/₂ in.)
Acquired 1934

Hodler was an individualist, and he made more portraits of himself than any other European painter except Rembrandt. *Self-portrait in a Stand-up Collar* was painted in the winter of 1879, after the artist had returned to Geneva from Madrid. It was the beginning of a hard time for him and this is strikingly reflected in this work. In spite of the elegant dress with an open-end tie and stand-up collar, and his well-groomed appearance with wavy hair, carefully combed and brushed mustache, and pointed beard, the facial expression, particularly the large, grey-green, questioning eyes, betrays a mood of uncertainty and skepticism. Something depressing is implied in the slight sideward twist of the upper body. This is the only example in the long series of Hodler's self-portraits of a diagonal figure composition. Moreover, it is worth noting that he has returned to the expressive chiaroscuro painting style of the early 1870s.

FERDINAND HODLER

Convalescent Woman

1879 or 1889
Oil on canvas
54 x 45 cm. (21 1/4 x 17 3/4 in.)

Convalescent Woman is among the most striking of the young Hodler's works: a woman sits in profile before her bed, her head slightly turned to the side, lost in thought. Her narrow face lies half in shadow which is brightened by subtle reflections. Her hands, marked by hard work, are toying with a randomly grasped garment. The picture is composed of a few large planes, bounded by gently flowing lines. The delicate coloring, the contrast of the black velvet dress to the milky pink of the coverlet, and the flesh color of the face are in keeping with the soft lineaments. *Convalescent Woman*, because of its psychological penetration and intensity of expression, permits comparison with Munch's *Sick Child* (1885–86; National Gallery, Oslo): Hodler probably misdated his own painting. Hodler, like both Van Gogh and Munch, belongs to a second generation whose early work showed a realistic phase.

FERDINAND HODLER

Ahasuerus

1886
Oil on canvas
104.5 x 81.5 cm. (41^{1}/$_{8}$ x 32^{1}/$_{16}$ in.)

Hodler repeatedly painted individuals who had borne heavy burdens in life: alcoholics, the destitute, the sick, and the aged.

The theme of *Ahasuerus* is directly related to the prose poem *Sosie* by Hodler's Geneva friend Louis Duchosal, who was called the "Swiss Verlaine." An old man without hope mourns his youthful years, which have flown by. He strides on restlessly: "I went, I had to go on, the Wandering Jew of Destiny ... how long the road; how weary I am!" says Duchosal's poem. And that is how Hodler presents *Ahasuerus*, symbol of the eternally homeless, shown against the light in an undefined landscape. The old man, lonely and weighed down with years, approaches the viewer directly. The lateral margins of the picture are brought parallel with the figure by means of his pilgrim's staff and the tree trunks.

Hodler, who all his life was confronted with dying and death, and who repeatedly presented this theme artistically, here depicts the man who cannot die: "You must wander unto the last day," the Jewish legend declares. Hodler may also have been inspired in his iconography by Gustave Doré's illustration *The Wandering Jew*. Later, he again drew on Doré; he painted a second version of *Ahasuerus*, around 1910 (private collection).

101

KARL HOFER

b. Karlsruhe, 1878
d. Berlin, 1955

Roman Self-Portrait

1906
Oil on canvas
44.5 x 42.5 cm. (17^1/$_2$ x 16^3/$_4$ in.)
Acquired by gift 1951

The Foundation owns eleven works by the German painter Karl Hofer from the years 1906–07. They testify to the artist's Roman sojourn (1903–08), which Theodor Reinhart had made possible. This grant committed the painter to leave a number of his pictures to his patron. With the assignment of these works to the Foundation, Oskar Reinhart established a memorial to his father's lifelong generosity.

This self-portrait, with its lightly applied paint and nuanced gradation of hues, seems, in contrast to Hofer's figure paintings of the time, more sketchy and spontaneous. Julius Meier-Graefe recognized it as the best work by Hofer thus far. Theodor Reinhart was also enthusiastic and on seeing it expressed the wish to sit for a portrait himself. Hofer agreed, and painted a *Portrait of Theodor Reinhart* in 1907, now in the Oskar Reinhart Foundation. Eleven years later, he portrayed him again in a canvas now owned by the Firma Gebr. Volkart, Winterthur.

103

The Oskar Reinhart Collection "Am Römerholz"

UPPER RHENISH MASTER

First quarter of the fifteenth century

Annunciation

Ca. 1420
Tempera on panel
18.5 x 14.8 cm. (7¼ x 5¹³/₁₆ in.)
Acquired 1927

The first part of the extraordinary selection of European paintings in the "Am Römerholz" collection is comprised of a number of works from the fifteenth and sixteenth centuries. This *Annunciation*, a jewel of delicate coloring, painted by a master from the Upper Rhine district, stands out among these. The picture is no larger than a man's hand and was probably painted by a miniaturist. He must have been one of the earliest northern artists to depict space in a rudimentary one-point perspective, thus producing a self-contained entity. The resulting distortions are charming. The objects in the foreground are of symbolic significance; for instance, the locked casket is an allusion to Mary's virginity; the boxwood tree refers to the Trinity, and the carnations to the future crucifixion of Christ.

The little picture is generally believed to have come from the region of the Upper Rhine. However, scholars are not quite unanimous as to its attribution to the Master of the Frankfurt Paradiesgärtlein, whose painting of paradise now hangs in the Städelsches Kunstinstitut, Frankfurt.

GERARD DAVID

b. Oudewater, ca. 1460
d. Bruges, 1523

Pietà

Ca. 1500–10
Tempera on panel
80 x 51.5 cm. (31$\frac{1}{2}$ x 20$\frac{1}{4}$ in.)
Acquired 1931

Toward the end of the fifteenth century, Gerard David, working in the tradition of Jan van Eyck, became the dominant personality among the artists of Bruges. His preference for graceful Gothic modelling of the human form and folds of drapery, which is especially evident in this *Pietà*, links his art with that of his precursors. His striving for clarity, the introspective mood of devotion, as well as a distinctly three-dimensional conception of space, the powerful and expressive representation of the landscape, and an elegant coolness of color in the broken green and blue tones—these are all characteristic of David's art. The theme of the Virgin Mary mourning over the body of Christ, the Pietà, appears repeatedly in the work of this artist. The Winterthur panel is similar to the central panel of an altarpiece in the Johnson Collection, Philadelphia. A weaker reworking of this theme, perhaps even a copy by someone else, is in the San Gil Church in Burgos. (Koella, *Sammlung Oskar Reinhart Am Römerholz.*)

107

MATTHIAS GRÜNEWALD

b. Würzburg, ca. 1470
d. Halle, 1528

Lamenting Woman with Folded Hands

Ca. 1512–16
Black chalk on yellow-brown paper
41 x 30 cm. (16^{1}/$_{8}$ x 11^{13}/$_{16}$ in.)
Acquired 1926

After Dürer, Grünewald is the most important representative of the art of painting north of the Alps at the turn of the fifteenth century. At the same time, he is Dürer's exact opposite. Dürer most impressively represented the classical art of the Renaissance in the North. Grünewald, in contrast, stands closer to late-medieval mysticism than to the rationalism of the dawning new age. He dedicated himself exclusively to painting. He never did woodcuts or engravings. His drawings, of which there are about forty, were intrinsic to his painting. This drawing is related to his work on the Isenheim altarpiece (ca. 1515; Musée d'Unterlinden, Colmar). Grünewald disregards all academic rules in order to heighten the expressive and ecstatic ardor of the figure. The same pose, with arms and hands fervently clasped, can be found again, almost unchanged, in Mary in the Crucifixion panel of the Isenheim altarpiece. At the same time, *Lamenting Woman* also shows a certain resemblance to the figure of the Isenheim Magdalene.

109

LUCAS CRANACH THE ELDER

b. Kronach, Upper Franconia, 1472
d. Weimar, 1553

Portrait of Dr. Johannes Cuspinian

Ca. 1502–03
Oil on panel
60 x 45 cm. (23⅝ x 17¾ in.)
Acquired 1925

Portrait of Anna Putsch

Ca. 1502–03
Oil on panel
60 x 45 cm. (23⅝ x 17¾ in.)
Acquired 1925

These portraits of the Viennese scholar Johannes Cuspinian and his wife, Anna Putsch, were painted by Lucas Cranach the Elder. They are among the artist's most famous works and formerly belonged to the English king Charles I.

At the time that the portraits were painted, Cuspinian (1473–1529) was a professor in the Medical School of the University of Vienna. He was one of the most important philosophers of German humanism. The massive book he holds here, with its gold lettering and seals, identifies him as a scholar. Cranach's pictorial method in this portrait derives from Italian models and perhaps to some extent from Dürer as well. (Koepplin, *Cranachs Ehebildnis des Johannes Cuspinian.*) The background has given rise to various interpretations: the figures probably represent signs of the Zodiac and characterize the subject. For example, Cuspinian is shown as a child of Saturn and therefore inclined to melancholy. This is indicated by the bright star (Saturn, the star of melancholy) above his head, and the owl (the bird of Saturn) in the sky. The small figures in the background allude to the contemplative, introspective nature of melancholy in their proclivity for solitude.

Anna Putsch (1485–1513) is depicted in an ornately trimmed dress and is shown as having been born under the sign of the Sun. This is indicated by the warm sunlight and the parrot and eagle, both of whom are regarded as birds of the sun. The hunting scene and the fire in the background suggest that Jupiter and Mars also play a role in the young woman's horoscope. In her right hand she holds a white carnation, symbol of virginity, and this indicates that these portraits were painted to commemorate the betrothal of the pair. The pictures must have been painted at the time of the couple's marriage, toward the end of 1502 or the beginning of 1503. As was then customary, the wife is sitting to the left of her husband. These two panels belong together, as the design makes clear. The backgrounds of both pictures form a continuous landscape; in one we find waters widening into a bay in the other, while in the foreground the two figures turn toward each other, framed by a symmetrical pair of trees.

HANS HOLBEIN THE YOUNGER

b. Augsburg, 1497/98
d. London, 1543

Portrait of Elizabeth Widmerpole

Ca. 1536–38
Resin tempera on panel
29.8 x 24.8 cm. (11³/4 x 9³/4 in.)
Acquired 1934

Hans Holbein, the son of an important late-Gothic painter of altarpieces, is among the most important representatives of German Renaissance art. His fame was initially based on the building facades he painted in Lucerne and Basel. He later became the most sought-after portraitist in England, not only by wealthy German merchants there, but also at the court of Henry VIII. His work is marked by a cool objectivity, clear line, and a monumental and stately character.

This portrait of Elizabeth Widmerpole is a companion piece to Holbein's portrait of John Godsalve (Philadelphia Museum of Art). Lady Elizabeth was the second wife of Godsalve, who was secretary and keeper of the seal in Thomas Cromwell's service. He was raised to the peerage in 1547. She appears sitting on a bench in elegant English dress, with pearls appliquéd along the edge of her cap. The color of the face and hands is light and cool; the lips are a pale pink. With the sureness of a master, Holbein has captured a socially assured yet modest personality. This portrait, which reminds one of a miniature, shows him at the height of his art.

PIETER BRUEGEL THE ELDER

b. Bruegel or Breda, 1525/30
d. Brussels, 1569

Adoration of the Magi
in the Snow

1567
Oil on panel
35 x 55 cm. (13¾ x 21⅝ in.)
Acquired 1930

Pieter Bruegel the Elder was also called "Peasant Bruegel". He painted fantastic peasant scenes, first-rate genre subjects and parables, as well as superb landscapes.

To discover what is happening in our painting, we are compelled to find our way through the driving snow, as do the figures in the picture themselves. We see the square of a village crowded with people. Only after much searching is it possible to find the scene of the Adoration in a hut at the left-hand edge of the panel. It is only one small part of the general action, concealed by the fact that Bruegel has shown it as though it were taking place in a Flemish village of his own time. This is not the earliest snowy Christmas picture—Altdorfer's *Holy Night* in the Vienna Kunsthistorisches Museum comes to mind—but the idea of showing the scene in a snowstorm probably originated in the calendar pictures in Flemish Books of Hours, which Bruegel used extensively as source material. (Koella, *Sammlung Oskar Reinhart Am Römerholz*.) In this painting he combined a profane genre scene, the snowy village, with a sacred one, the Adoration. Most of the various copies of this picture were done by his eldest son, Pieter Bruegel the Younger.

EL GRECO

b. Candia, Crete, 1541
d. Toledo, 1614

Portrait of the Inquisitor Cardinal Don Fernando Niño de Guevara

Ca. 1600
Oil on canvas
74 x 51 cm. (29^1/$_8$ x 20^1/$_{16}$ in.)
Acquired 1924

Niño de Guevara, who was born in Toledo in 1541, was appointed Cardinal in 1596 and Inquisitor in 1600. Named Archbishop of Seville in 1601, he died in 1609. His remains were transferred to the Church of San Pablo in Toledo in 1611. The half-length portrait of the Cardinal-Inquisitor by El Greco shows this, the most powerful and feared man in the Spanish Church of 1600, clad in the purple and crowned with his biretta. The narrow face gives an impression of asceticism; the features are hard, forbidding, and bony. The piercing eyes peer watchfully from behind spectacles; the lips are pressed firmly together. This pitiless expression is emphasized by the cut of the beard and mustache. The portrait is probably a preliminary study for the famous full-length portrait of the Cardinal and Grand Inquisitor at the Metropolitan Museum, New York; alternatively, it may be a partial reproduction made by the painter himself a few years later.

This painting inspired the German writer Stefan Andres (1906–70) to write the short story, *El Greco malt den Grossinquisitor* (1936).

116

117

PETER PAUL RUBENS

b. Siegen, Westphalia, 1577
d. Antwerp, 1640

The Consul Decius Mus Consults the Augurs

1617
Oil on panel
74 x 104 cm. (29^{1}/$_{8}$ x 40^{15}/$_{16}$ in.)
Acquired 1954

Rubens's loosely painted tapestry sketch, *The Consul Decius Mus Consults the Augurs*, fits perfectly into the concept of the "Am Römerholz" collection. Rubens based this picture on an anecdote by the Roman historian Livy. Decius Mus had dreamt of two hostile armies, and that either the General or his army would have to be sacrificed to the gods of the underworld. He told his dream to the Augurs, and when the results of their sacrifice confirmed the dream, Decius Mus decided to give his own life to save his army and ensure a victory for Rome. Rubens was commissioned by a Genoese noble (probably Niccolò Pallavicini) to depict this theme in a set of seven pictures; the draft at Winterthur shows the second of these scenes. A painting that was executed from this preparatory sketch is currently in the collection of the Prince of Liechtenstein in Vaduz. It is this painting that was finally used for the cartoon for the tapestry manufactured by the Brussels weavers.

119

NICOLAS POUSSIN

b. Villers, Les Andelys, 1594
d. Rome, 1665

The Holy Family

Ca. 1635–37
Oil on canvas
87 x 66 cm. (34¹/₄ x 26 in.)
Acquired 1925

In the Reinhart Collection, French painting begins with the Baroque painters Poussin and Claude Lorrain, who hold the position in French classical painting that Corneille and Racine hold in literature. They painted themes from mythology set in classical landscapes, and depicted episodes from the Bible. Poussin's *Holy Family* occupied a central position in his oeuvre. This narrative painting originates in an apocryphal tradition, the so-called childhood gospels. It shows the Holy Family pausing to rest during the flight into Egypt, a popular subject in the sixteenth and seventeenth centuries, and one also seen in works by Correggio, Barocci, and Caravaggio. (Voss, "Die Flucht nach Aegypten.") In opposition to these painters, Poussin changed the theme into a classical arrangement. The Holy Family is shown sitting near an ancient temple. Cherubs bow down to offer the Infant Jesus fruit and garlands. The composition and warm coloring betray the influence of Venetian painting.

120

121

JEAN-BAPTISTE SIMEON CHARDIN

b. Paris, 1699
d. Paris, 1779

Crystal Bowl and Fruit

Ca. 1758–59
Oil on canvas
37 x 45.5 cm. (14⁹/₁₆ x 17¹⁵/₁₆ in.)

Eighteenth-century French painting is represented in the Winterthur collection by pictures by Watteau, Fragonard, and Boucher, as well as a number of important works by Jean-Baptiste Siméon Chardin. Chardin, a member of the French bourgeoisie, painted prior to the Revolution. He is considered a painter-poet and occupies a position between Vermeer and Corot. He is particularly famous for his enchanting still lifes. "What a painter! What a master of color! The objects seem to emerge from the canvas and partake of a reality that deceives the eye," wrote Denis Diderot, publisher of the great French Encyclopaedia in *Oeuvres esthétiques*. How very true. In this painting even the fuzz on the peach skins is faithfully reproduced.

Such still lifes, with their simple composition and their charm, continued to influence succeeding generations of artists, including Cézanne, Matisse, and Morandi—to name only a few.

FRANCESCO GUARDI

b. Venice, 1712
d. Venice, 1793

Venice: Riva degli Schiavoni

Ca. 1780–90
Oil on canvas
34 x 40.5 cm. (13³/₈ x 15¹⁵/₁₆ in.)
Acquired 1912

The Venetian Francesco Guardi was a genius in the use of color. While Canaletto recorded the buildings and monuments of Venice with precision, Guardi evoked the enchanting aura of that city. Already in the late fifteenth century, its towers and domes, "hovering twixt sky and sea," can be found in paintings, though at that time they served solely as landmarks or background. (See, for example, Gentile Bellini's *Procession at the Piazza San Marco*, 1496; Gallerie dell'Accademia, Venice.)

Venice came into its own as a subject for paintings only after landscape painting became generally emancipated during the seventeenth century. The work here shows a view of the Riva degli Schiavoni. In the center we see the Piazzetta, the Libreria, and the Doges' Palace, the old Campanile, and the domes of San Marco. To the left, on the water and bisected by the edge of the canvas, is the Venetian State Barge. This is a late Guardi work and its finely shaded coloring expresses the romantic, slightly decayed character of Venice and evokes the melancholy of the ephemeral.

FRANCISCO JOSÉ DE GOYA

b. Fuente de Todos, Spain, 1746
d. Bordeaux, 1828

The Washerwomen

Ca. 1779
Oil on canvas
86.5 x 59 cm. (34^1/$_{16}$ x 23^1/$_4$ in.)
Acquired 1955

There is no doubt that Goya's work serves as the focal point of Spanish painting at Winterthur. He is represented by six works, some of them of great importance. There are portraits, still lifes, and two drafts for tapestry cartoons depicting scenes from everyday life, and hinting at the artist's interest in Tiepolo. Card players are shown in one of these sketches; in the other, washerwomen. The tapestry with the washerwomen motif was intended for the anteroom of the princes of Asturias in the Prado; today it is in the Escorial. Another cartoon, the same size as the tapestry, is hung in the Prado Museum. It lay ready for execution in January 1780 at the Royal tapestry workshops.

The Washerwomen is among the best works Goya created in the first part of his career. Five young women are seen near some drying laundry in an idyllic eighteenth-century landscape. While one carries a bundle of laundry on her head, the others are resting. Two are playing with a sheep, a third is sleeping, leaning against her neighbor.

127

FRANCISCO JOSÉ DE GOYA

Still Life with Salmon

Ca. 1808–12
Oil on canvas
45 x 62 cm. (17³/₄ x 24³/₈ in.)
Acquired 1937

Goya's still lifes frequently portray dead animals, in which the macabre aspect of death is predominant. The *Still Life with Salmon* is undoubtedly one of Goya's most mature works, for he contrives here to conjure up a mysterious, and indeed demonic, effect from his simple subject. Three slices of salmon, lying on a great table before a black background, are arranged to form a self-contained group. The cut flesh is red, the sinews white, pink, and yellow, and the dark sections covered with clotted blood are painted deep brown and reddish brown.

The picture reveals something demoniacal and horrible which usually finds expression in Goya's figure paintings—such as *The Execution of the Rebels on the Third of May, 1808* (1814; Prado, Madrid) and the contemporaneous cycle of etchings entitled *The Disasters of War.*

128

FRANCISCO JOSÉ DE GOYA

Portrait of Don José Pio de Molina

Ca. 1827–28
Oil on canvas
60.5 x 50 cm. (23¹³/₁₆ x 19¹¹/₁₆ in.)

Goya painted relatively few portraits in the last years of his life. At this time he was occupied mostly with drawings, miniatures, and lithographs. He took up his brush only for a few friends and for his nephew Mariano.

Almost all of Goya's late works impart an enigmatic sensation of menace, as is shown by the portrait of Don José Pio de Molina, one of the artist's last works. This unfinished portrait is composed in red and near-black tones. The face, with its sunken features, expresses all the bitterness of the exile, the soul's suffering that both he and the artist endured. De Molina was one of the painter's closest friends and provided him with a home when he was exiled in Bordeaux in 1824.

At that time, many Spanish exiles had sought refuge in Bordeaux: writers, artists, businessmen, politicians, bankers. It is said that De Molina was present when Goya died.

JOHN CONSTABLE

b. East Bergholt, Suffolk, 1776
d. London, 1837

Hampstead Heath

1824
Oil on canvas
60 x 77 cm. (23⁵/₈ x 30⁵/₁₆ in.)
Acquired 1932

John Constable and William Turner are the foremost figures in English landscape painting. At first Constable was strongly influenced by the seventeenth-century artists Ruisdael and Claude Lorraine. In the period that followed, he devoted himself to the direct study of nature, creating remarkable landscapes: "For the last two years I have been running after pictures, and seeking the truth at second hand. . . . I shall return to Bergholt, where I shall endeavor to get a pure and unaffected manner of representing the scenes that may employ me." (Leslie, *Memoirs of the Life of John Constable*.) Constable followed his goal of "embodying a pure apprehension of natural effect."

The Winterthur picture is one of a series of landscapes that Constable painted near Hampstead. He had rented a house there in 1819 in the hope that the fresh air would be beneficial for his wife's health. He liked the area so much that he moved there permanently and eventually bought a house in Hampstead, which he owned until his death.

Our painting depicts a favorite theme of the artist: The view of the sand quarries near Branch Hill Lake, which were constantly bustling with horses and wagons. In a letter dated August 1, 1825, Constable describes this precise piece of landscape, although he is probably referring to another version of this picture: "A scene on Hampstead Heath, with broken foreground and sand carts, Windsor Castle in the extreme distance on the right of the shower. The fresh greens in the distance (which you are pleased to admire) are the fields about Harrow, and the village of Hendon, Kilburn &c." (Constable, *Correspondence*.) Delacroix was also fascinated by Constable's painting of greens—he wrote in his diary: "Constable says that the superiority of the green in his meadows is a result of the fact that it is composed of a number of different greens. The green of the ordinary landscape painters has so little intensity because they handle it as a single tone. What he says about the green of the meadows can be applied to all the other color tones as well." (Lankheit, *Revolution und Restauration*.)

Constable interpreted the sky, with its mountain ranges of clouds, with the intensity characteristic of all his work. He wrote in 1821: "That landscape painter who does not make his skies a very material part of his composition, neglects to avail himself of one of his greatest aids." (Leslie, *Memoirs*.) Moreover, Constable painted a whole series of cloud studies and was the first artist to use moving clouds as the sole subjects of oil paintings.

Not surprisingly, Constable's work had a great influence upon the painters of the Barbizon school.

131

JEAN AUGUSTE DOMINIQUE INGRES

b. Montauban, 1780
d. Paris, 1867

Portrait of an Unknown Lady

1816
Crayon
20.6 x 15.9 cm. (8¹/₈ x 6¹/₄ in.)

Even those who have reservations about Ingres's austerely constructed Christian, mythological, and historical pictures cannot deny that his portraits deserve high admiration. His native talent for the keen observation of reality and the unique sensitivity of his line establish him as one of the greatest graphic portraitists ever. In his own words, "To draw does not mean simply to reproduce contours; drawing does not consist merely of line: drawing is also expression, the inner form, the plane, the modelling. . . . With the exception of hue, drawing contains everything." (Ingres, *Du dessin*.)

The portrait of a lady shown here was drawn in 1816 in Rome. There, Ingres made portraits of a whole series of foreigners, especially English and French nationals. In this way he was able to support himself after his former clients, the French functionaries in Rome, had left following the collapse of the Napoleonic Empire. Today, the woman portrayed in the Winterthur drawing cannot be identified. Nevertheless, her individuality is unquestionable, brought out partly in soft, partly in hard strokes. The face has been worked out in detail; elsewhere the lines have been summarily applied.

JEAN AUGUSTE DOMINIQUE INGRES

Portrait of Madame Ingres-Ramel

1859
Oil on canvas
63 x 50 cm. (24^{13}/$_{16}$ x 19^{11}/$_{16}$ in.)
Acquired 1924

Ingres's wife, Madeleine Chapelle, died in 1849. Three years later, taking the advice of his friends, the seventy-two-year-old artist decided to marry forty-four-year-old Delphine Ramel (1808–87) at Versailles. She was related to Ingres's friend Marcotte, president and later director of the Paris Ecole des Beaux-Arts. This portrait was painted in 1859 as a companion piece to the self-portrait now in the Uffizi. It derives its special quality from the precise draftsmanship and the subtle, fresh application of color, particularly in the skin, clothing, and jewelry. But it is the expression of the face that is noteworthy: it bespeaks great nobility and sensibility. Soft, round lines define this portrait, which is stamped by a devotion to beauty.

A preparatory drawing, slightly different from the Winterthur picture, is in the Fogg Art Museum, Harvard University.

135

THEODORE GERICAULT

b. Rouen, 1791
d. Paris, 1824

***A Madman with
    Military Delusions***

Ca. 1819–24
Oil on canvas
81 x 65 cm. (31$^7/_8$ x 25$^5/_8$ in.)

Representation of the mentally ill came into vogue in the eighteenth century. The Englishman Hogarth, in *The Rake's Progress*, and the Spaniard Goya depicted scenes from insane asylums in impressive works. Géricault, himself mentally unstable and influenced by the Paris alienist Dr. Georget, painted a number of pictures of the mentally ill. They are among the most important examples of this type of painting. Five such portraits have been preserved. Five additional ones are mentioned in the literature, but all trace of them has been lost. Dr. Georget published his dissertation on insanity and its causes under the title *De la folie*. He believed that it was possible to draw conclusions about psychic illnesses from facial characteristics. It is probable that the portraits were intended as demonstration material for his lectures. The *Madman with Military Delusions* is shown against a dark background. He wears a white shirt and a black vest. A coat is thrown over his right shoulder. There is a medal on his chest and he wears a field hat with a red tassel. His face is brightly lighted on one side; the other lies in deep shadow, so that the face is sharply bisected. This increases the impression of madness, of unreality. The flesh is iridescent, with a lively play of colors. The eyes glance sideways, and the lips are pressed together, lending the man a glassy stare and a grim and distrustful expression.

There is some dispute about the exact dates of these *Madman* portraits, but it is likely that they range between 1819 and 1824.

137

JEAN-BAPTISTE CAMILLE COROT

b. Paris, 1796
d. Paris, 1875

Young Girl Reading

Ca. 1855–60
Oil on canvas
46 x 38.5 cm. (18^{1}/$_{8}$ x 15^{1}/$_{8}$ in.)
Acquired 1938

Of the nine works by Corot in the "Am Römerholz" collection, six are landscapes and three are figure paintings. The artist preferred to be recognized as a landscape painter. His figures, which gradually became known after his death in 1875, are with few exceptions paintings of women; he rarely painted a group, and never a couple. They are presented as half-length or three-quarter-length portraits; full-length figures are exceptions. Equally rare are representations of nudes. Corot depicts his models in meditative poses: reading, holding a mandolin, dreaming, gazing at a picture, or simply sitting or standing. Individuality unfolds in the type; the figures hold the middle ground between portrait and genre. In them Vermeer and Chardin live on. The theme of the reading girl appears in Corot's work in the late 1840s, and the first version of it is set in an interior (Bührle Collection, Zurich). In our picture, the girl is sitting in an open landscape under a grey, cloudy sky. In the right background there are sheep grazing. The cool, controlled palette in silver-grey tones is characteristic of Corot's style.

139

JEAN-BAPTISTE CAMILLE COROT

Château-Thierry

Ca. 1855–65
Oil on canvas
38 x 55.5 cm. (15 x 21⁷/₈ in.)
Acquired 1936

Camille Corot often painted in Château-Thierry, a town northeast of Paris; here he depicts it in an overall view, as seen from the left bank of the Marne. The houses, mirrored only indistinctly in the leaden grey surface of the broad, sluggish stream, appear a subdued white and grey. The earthen, greyish-brown left bank slopes away gently. The washerwoman at the water's edge and the two other women on the road almost disappear, absorbed by the landscape. An overcast sky arches over all, in soft, subtle neutral shades. Thus Corot, with his characteristic silvery-cool palette, has evoked a peaceful, dreamy mood, creating a picture "full of serene melancoly" (Holz, "Sein ist Farbe—Die Sammlung Oskar Reinhart").

Corot himself commented on the meaning of this mood in his paintings. "Beauty in art is truth bathed in an impression received from nature. I am struck upon seeing a certain place. While I strive for conscious imitation, I never for an instant lose the emotion that has taken hold of me. Reality is one part of art; feeling completes it." (Moreau-Nélaton, *Corot raconté par lui-même*.)

JEAN-BAPTISTE CAMILLE COROT

Dunkirk Harbor

1873
Oil on canvas
40 x 55.5 cm. (15³/₄ x 21⁷/₈ in.)
Acquired 1948

This small harbor picture was created by Corot two years before his death. It was painted while he was at Dunkirk, with the spontaneous brushstrokes of his late style. As in *Château-Thierry* (see page 141), this painting is evidence of Corot's unique method of rendering atmosphere and light. In the preceding picture, the sluggishly flowing stream dominates a horizontal composition; in this one, Corot is more concerned with painting the still water. The vertical accents in *Dunkirk Harbor* also are markedly stronger, and the figures are given more prominence.

EUGENE DELACROIX

b. Charenton-Saint-Maurice, France,
   1798
d. Paris, 1863

Scene from the Greek Wars of Independence

Ca. 1827
Oil on canvas
65 x 81 cm. (25⅝ x 31⅞ in.)
Acquired 1921

Delacroix is represented in the "Am Römerholz" collection by eleven works, assembled by Oskar Reinhart from various periods of the artist's development. Two of them document his involvement with the Greek struggle for liberty. One picture is an allegory: *Greece Expiring on the Ruins of Missolonghi* (ca. 1826). Directly alluding to an ode by Byron, the artist depicted Greece as a young woman. Byron had died at Missolonghi in 1822, during the second siege of the town. His poems were an important source of pictorial subjects for Delacroix, and *Scene from the Greek Wars of Independence* shares a kindred spirit with the Romantic works of the poet. The painting, like an eyewitness account, dramatically documents European sympathy with the Greek movement for independence from the Turks.

The impassioned battle is expressed with artistic creativity by Delacroix through three figures: the fallen soldier on the ground, the galloping horseman, and the third soldier, whose horse has been killed, firing his weapon. Clouds of gunpowder intensify the drama of the scene.

145

EUGENE DELACROIX

Tasso in the Insane Asylum

1839
Oil on canvas
60 x 50 cm. (23^5/$_8$ x 19^{11}/$_{16}$ in.)
Acquired 1919

Delacroix repeatedly dealt with themes from literature. He visualized tragic episodes from the works of Dante, Goethe, Shakespeare, Walter Scott, and above all Byron, in ever new variations.

Very early on, he became preoccupied with the figure of the Italian poet Torquato Tasso (1544–95). The Winterthur picture, painted in 1839, shows Tasso sitting apathetically in his cell, exposed to the mockery and curiosity of the sensation seekers on the other side of the bars. One of them stretches out his arm toward the papers lying on the couch, as though he would like to know what is written on them. Other pages have fluttered onto the floor. Tasso symbolizes the lonely, misunderstood artist. This mood is communicated through differentiated green and brown tones, as well as in the lighting.

This picture is among the most striking of Delacroix's achievements. Charles Baudelaire dedicated the sonnet *Sur le Tasse en prison* to him; Théophile Gautier also described it; and, in a letter written to his brother Theo in 1888, Vincent van Gogh referred to it as a model painting.

147

EUGENE DELACROIX

Tobias and the Angel

1863
Oil on canvas
40.5 x 32.5 cm. ($15^{15}/_{16}$ x $12^{13}/_{16}$ in.)

Delacroix had taken up the theme of *Tobias and the Angel* before 1863, but not in original compositions. Rather, he had made two copies, based on works by Titian and Rembrandt. This small picture, Delacroix's last work, was not primarily designed to tell the biblical story. Instead, it was to recreate a mood: the stillness and isolation of a secluded area near the river. Thus, the artist painted the landscape in the most gentle tones. A soft web of silvery grey veils the green of the water and the earth. From this, the red figure of Tobias and the blue of the angel emerge. In such a poetic interpretation, Delacroix comes close to his contemporary Corot.

149

HONORE DAUMIER

b. Marseilles, 1808
d. Valmondois, 1879

Don Quixote Turns a Somersault for Sancho Panza

Ca. 1850–55
Charcoal
34.5 x 25 cm. (13⁹/₁₆ x 9⁷/₈ in.)

Oskar Reinhart allocated a separate gallery to Daumier, who is represented in the collection by an especially rich selection of twenty paintings, watercolors, and drawings.

It is not by chance that we have come to know Daumier chiefly as a caricaturist. His enormous graphic oeuvre—Delteil's catalogue lists about 4,000 works—has been widely distributed. But above all, it is the vivid quality of his creations that assured him preeminence in this field of art—whether he dealt with themes from politics, everyday life, or literature. Literature especially played an important role in Daumier's work. He repeatedly delved into his favorite books for source material, and attended the theater with great enthusiasm. Much of what he read and saw was echoed in his work. He was inspired by Homer and Greek mythology, by La Fontaine, Molière, and Cervantes.

Daumier felt a particularly deep affinity for Cervantes's *Don Quixote*. He interpreted the tragicomic epic in numerous oil paintings, watercolors, and charcoal drawings, although it never appeared as a theme in the lithographs that were intended for the general public. He was unique in his ability to translate and interpret the meaning of a literary idea into the language of the visual. Daumier follows the two protagonists, Don Quixote—the knightly idealist and avenger of all injustice—and his servant Sancho Panza—the pragmatist—through all their adventures.

The Reinhart Collection owns three works from this cycle, two oil paintings and this drawing, which is among the most splendid creations of the artist. It shows Don Quixote—dressed only in a shirt—turning a somersault to demonstrate his passion for Dulcinea to Sancho Panza, who refuses to watch his master's folly.

150

151

HONORE DAUMIER

The Return from the Market

Ca. 1855–57
Oil on canvas
35 x 28 cm. (13¾ x 11 in.)
Acquired 1936

From the 1840s on, Daumier turned more and more toward painting, and away from popular lithography. The writer Champfleury was convinced that the establishment of the French Republic in 1830, which did not seem to offer Daumier the caricaturist any more subject matter, was responsible for the artist's turning to painting. This extremely questionable assumption must remain hypothetical. However, it is unarguable that Daumier's paintings, which until recently have remained a largely neglected chapter of art history, rank in their originality and quality with the lithographs.

The Return from the Market is an example of Daumier's high painterly quality and advanced creative technique. With the most economical of means he has achieved a maximum of effect and reduced the subject to its simplest form. It is extraordinary how the decorative style of flat planes works powerfully with the contrast of bright and dark. Here Daumier has dispensed completely with the representation of details. Stylistically, this painting is closely related to *The Good Samaritan* (Glasgow Art Gallery and Museum).

HONORE DAUMIER

Children Bathing

Ca. 1855–57
Oil on panel
24.5 x 33 cm. (9⅝ x 13 in.)
Acquired 1936

The poet Charles Baudelaire wrote of his contemporary Daumier: "Leaf through his work and before your eyes a fantastic and fascinating world will come to life: this multicolored life of our big city. He has perceived everything, all the shocking, grotesque, depressing and amusing elements that are concealed in her." (*Curiosités esthétiques*.)

At that time, Daumier lived on the Ile St.-Louis, in the heart of Paris. Here he observed the life of the ordinary people in the streets. The small picture *Children Bathing*, which belongs in the long series of representations of everyday life in Paris, comes into being in this context. It was calculated to emphasize the contrast between light and dark, and in its composition reveals an inner monumentality. "This fellow embodies Michelangelo," said Balzac, whose themes in many respects resemble those of Daumier. Both created a profound "*comédie humaine*"; conversely, the painter Daubigny, standing in the Sistine Chapel, cried out, "That is just as though it were by Daumier." (Fleischmann, *Honoré Daumier.*)

153

HONORE DAUMIER

The Two Doctors and Death

Ca. 1865–69
Chalk, pen, and watercolor
32.5 x 28 cm. (12^{13}/$_{16}$ x 11 in.)
Acquired 1922

154

Daumier felt himself drawn toward La Fontaine through an inner sense of kinship. Thus, now and again, one finds themes from the latter's fables in the artist's work. Our drawing is among these; it is an illustration for the *Two Doctors*, a satire on the conceit and charlatanry of physicians. Arrogant and vain, leaning over backward, each is trying to prove to the other with excessive gesticulations that his diagnosis is the right one. Yet, while the two are energetically discussing the matter in the foreground, in the background Death carries off the patient, reducing their debate to mere rhetoric.

HONORE DAUMIER

Pierrot Playing the Mandolin

Ca. 1873
Oil on panel
35 x 26.5 cm. (13³/4 x 10⁷/16 in.)
Acquired 1928

In the last decade of his life, when Daumier was in his seventies, he seldom turned to painting, since his sight was becoming ever weaker. Since 1873, he had been living in Valmondois, a small village forty kilometers northwest of Paris. The painter Camille Corot, a helpful friend, gave him a summer house there as a gift.

Pierrot Playing the Mandolin is one of his last works, and its effect is like that of a magical echo or reminiscence of French painting of the eighteenth century. In its theme, this small picture recalls Watteau; in its sketchlike technique, using powerful brushstrokes rapidly dashed off, it recalls Fragonard. On the other hand, it also anticipates the Expressionism of the twentieth century in its style, which resembles that of Kokoschka.

157

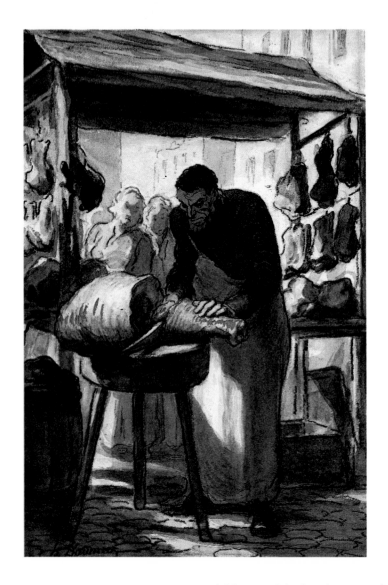

HONORE DAUMIER

The Butcher

Chalk, pen, ink, and watercolor
washes
30 x 20.2 cm. (11 ¹³/₁₆ x 7 ¹⁵/₁₆ in.)

158

The powerful figure of the butcher, raised from the mundane to the timeless, is one of several occupational types that Daumier often represented. The theme appears in several variations. In the present drawing, the gruesome aspect of butchering is emphasized, making one think of Goya. Not coincidentally, the French writer Champfleury wrote in his *Histoire de la caricature moderne*: "There exist hidden similarities between the Spaniard and the man from Marseilles."

HONORE DAUMIER

The Third-Class Railway Carriage

Chalk, pen, and watercolor, highlighted with white
23 x 33 cm. (9$\frac{1}{16}$ x 13 in.)
Acquired 1923

The railroad, still new in Daumier's lifetime, occupied an important place in his work. In a series of lithographs he depicted the little adventures and comic incidents which Parisians experienced on their first train rides. He also made drawings and paintings that convey a more serious, almost depressing mood. Daumier liked to choose interiors of waiting rooms or third-class train compartments, and with full social consciousness represented characteristic types of people. In the Winterthur drawing, a child is sleeping on the hard bench; men and women stare dully before them or doze off; others gaze out the window or try to shorten the journey through conversation. The faces and postures of these people create the impression that they are on an endless journey. The train ride becomes a metaphor for life.

GUSTAVE COURBET

b. Ornans, France, 1819
d. La Tour de Peilz, Switzerland,
   1877

The Hammock

1844
Oil on canvas
70.5 x 97 cm. (27³/₄ x 38³/₁₆ in.)
Acquired 1924

This painting shows a young woman lying in a hammock in a grottolike wooded landscape. As a study for it in a private collection shows, Courbet had been concerned with this theme since 1839. In that work the girl is shown nude, and the scene seems strongly influenced by the erotic charm of the Rococo. The Winterthur painting, on the other hand, turns this Rococo idyll into a contemporary reality. The girl is now dressed in ordinary, everyday clothes, although her uncovered bosom created quite a stir at the time. Water, grottos, dreaming, and sleep are important leitmotifs in the work of Courbet. Details like leaves, fabric patterns, and hair are precisely reproduced by this outstanding Realist. The girl reminds one of the dreaming women of the German Romantics Schwind and Richter. The subject of the woman in the hammock recurs later on in German painting in the work of Thoma—although he handles it in a totally different way (1876; Städelsches Kunstinstitut, Frankfurt).

161

GUSTAVE COURBET

The Wave

1870
Oil on canvas
80.5 x 99.5 cm. (31^{11}/$_{16}$ x 39^{3}/$_{16}$ in.)
Acquired 1925

Cézanne described Courbet as "a great painter of people. And of Nature." (*Ueber die Kunst*.) In this connection, he made special mention of *The Wave*, one of the great seascapes produced by the artist around 1870. "It is as though it were coming straight for you, it makes you flinch," wrote Cézanne, and indeed this breaker, with its crown of spume, seems to be possessed of gigantic force as it surges in toward the beach indicated in the foreground. Yet Courbet needed only a few colors—green, grey, and brown—to capture the atmosphere of storm.

Courbet began to paint these pictures of ocean waves during a stay in Etretat, Normandy, in 1869. Since Courbet could not make the trip to the sea in 1870 because of the outbreak of the Franco-Prussian War, the versions painted later, including the Winterthur picture, were finished in his studio, or were painted entirely from memory. In Etretat, he had lived in the house of the landscape painter Eugène Le Poittevin, a relative of the writer Guy de Maupassant. Thus the latter observed the painter at work and wrote: "In a large empty room a gigantic, dirty, paint-smeared man pressed flecks of white paint onto a large empty canvas with a kitchen knife. From time to time he stepped to the window, pressed his face against the pane and gazed out into the storm. The sea came so close, as if it wanted to strike the house, which was plunged into the foam and uproar. The dirty water struck the window panes like hail and dripped down the walls." ("La Vie d'un paysagiste.") Maupassant's description corresponds exactly to Cézanne's perceptions. The public of the time was aware that political ideas could be associated with Courbet's wave pictures as well. The sea has frequently been used in France as a metaphor for the People. Thus, given Courbet's strong republican sympathies, one may discern in this canvas an implied defeat of the Empire by the overwhelming wave of a popular uprising. (*Courbet und Deutschland*, no. 288.)

CAMILLE PISSARRO

b. St. Thomas, Virgin Islands, 1830
d. Paris, 1903

**_Pontoise: A View
of the Hermitage_**

1874
Oil on canvas
61 x 81 cm. (24 x 31$^{7/8}$ in.)
Acquired 1923

In 1872, after returning from London, whither he had fled to escape the turmoil of the Franco-Prussian War, Pissarro settled in Pontoise, a small town northwest of Paris. Cézanne was also staying there at the time, in order to work closely with Pissarro, who had at last achieved an impressionistic technique. For him, Monet's influence had replaced that of Corot. In London, he had come to know the work of Constable and Turner. The light, loose brushstrokes of this painting show the change quite clearly.

At Pontoise, Pissarro found his themes in the village's narrow streets, peopled by country folk, and in the surrounding gardens screened by vines, where people sowed, hoed, and harvested. He especially liked to work in the vicinity of the Hermitage with its fruit and vegetable gardens.

"Don't proceed according to rules and principles, but paint what you observe and feel. Paint generously and unhesitatingly, for it is best not to lose the first impression. Don't be timid in front of nature: one must be bold, at the risk of being deceived and making mistakes. One must have only one master—nature; she is the one always to be consulted."

These words of Pissarro, which Louis Le Bail, a young man of his acquaintance, wrote down, summarize some essential ideas of Impressionist landscape painting. (Rewald, _The History of Impressionism_.)

164

165

EDOUARD MANET

b. Paris, 1832
d. Paris, 1883

At the Café

1878
Oil on canvas
78 x 84 cm. (30³/₄ x 33¹/₁₆ in.)
Acquired 1953

Manet is represented in the "Am Römerholz" collection by four works hung on a single wall. This large cafe scene, showing people drinking beer in the Paris brasserie *Cabaret de Reichshoffen* on the Boulevard Rochechouart, is a major picture by the master.

It took Oskar Reinhart thirty years to obtain this work. The room shown is the same as that in the two versions of the *Servante de Bock*, one now in the London National Gallery, the other in the Louvre. The young woman in a hat in the foreground is the well-known actress Ellen Andrée, and the bearded man next to her is the engraver Henri Guérard. The few figures are placed in such a way as to suggest a bustling, overcrowded room. In the background there is a mirror-image of a poster for the famous *Hanlon Lees* troupe of clowns, who were appearing at the Folies-Bergère at the time. Although at first sight the picture gives the impression of a snapshot, on closer inspection it is seen to be tightly composed of verticals, horizontals, and heavily emphasized diagonals, which bind the work into a compact entity. While it seems so fresh as to be a study from life, this picture was actually painted in the studio from pencil sketches.

167

EDOUARD MANET

A Bouquet of Flowers

Ca. 1882–83
Oil on canvas
54 x 34.5 cm. (24^1/$_4$ x 13^9/$_{16}$ in.)
Acquired 1923

Manet, a contemporary of the Impressionists, influenced them profoundly with his sketchlike painting technique. This work, with its spontaneous brushwork and delicate coloring, shows Manet's still-life art at a high point—a true marvel of color. It is one in a series of flower still lifes which the artist created in the last years of his life, when he was already seriously ill. He used the same crystal vase in other flower pictures painted in those years.

EDGAR DEGAS

b. Paris, 1834
d. Paris, 1917

Portrait of Giulietta Bellelli

Ca. 1857
Black chalk
26 x 18 cm. (10¼ x 7¹/₁₆ in.)
Acquired 1934

Portrayed here is Giulietta Bellelli, the younger daughter of Baron Bellelli, an Italian senator and friend of the statesman Cavour. Bellelli's wife, Laura Degas, was the artist's aunt. Giulietta, who was born in Naples in 1851, was six years old when this drawing was made. It is a study for the large painting of the *Bellelli Family* which today hangs in the Louvre. It is one of the most important family portraits of the nineteenth century. Degas spent several years on this group portrait: the first sketches were made in 1856 in Naples; later ones were done in Florence in subsequent years. He finished the painting only in 1862 in Paris. In the subtle delineation of this study one can recognize Degas's superb draftsmanship. A similar head study of Giulietta Bellelli is now in the Louvre.

EDGAR DEGAS

Dancer in Her Dressing Room

Ca. 1878–79
Pastel on cardboard
60 x 40 cm. (23⅝ x 15¾ in.)
Acquired 1923

Theater and ballet occupied a predominant position in Degas's artistic work, as did horseraces, milliners, and women at their toilette. Yet what interested him most was the action that occurred behind the scenes—the rehearsals and the wardrobe preparations that preceded the entrance on stage. Degas, however, did not paint his ballet scenes on the spot; he completed them in his studio on the basis of sketches made in the theater. This feature distinguishes him from the true Impressionists, who worked directly from nature. Degas himself agreed: "No art is less spontaneous than mine." (Hüttinger, *Degas*.) Nevertheless, the onlooker is fascinated by the immediate effect of his art.

In this picture, the viewer surprises a dancer trying on her costume in a flood of artificial light. The half-open door reinforces a suggestion of voyeurism.

ALFRED SISLEY

b. Paris, 1839
d. Moret-sur-Loing, 1899

Barges on the St.-Martin Canal

1870
Oil on canvas
54.5 x 73 cm. (21$^7/_{16}$ x 28$^3/_4$ in.)
Acquired 1923

The programmatic Impressionism of Sisley, Pissarro, and Monet reached its consummation in landscape painting. The artists worked directly from nature, allowing the time of day and of year, and the momentary atmosphere to determine the mood of the composition.

Sisley, born in Paris of English parents, did not begin as an artist, but first embraced a commercial career. When he turned to painting, he remained the most objective of the Impressionists. Each of his pictures, in contrast especially to the later works of Monet, has a definite pictorial space which never totally dissolves in atmosphere. Cool brightness and serenity characterize his paintings. In his early, impressionistic *St.-Martin Canal* he captured the charming atmosphere of a view of Paris. The humid air over the canal and the play of light on the water take on a quality of permanence that belies the lightness of the brushwork.

This picture is one of the most beautiful works by Sisley. The art historian Lionello Venturi calls it a true "miracle of color." (*Impressionists and Symbolists.*)

175

CLAUDE MONET

b. Paris, 1840
d. Giverny, 1926

Ice Floes on the Seine

1881
Oil on canvas
60 x 99 cm. (23⅝ x 39 in.)
Acquired 1924

Between 1880 and 1882 Monet painted a series of winter scenes near Vétheuil, all of them showing the Seine in flood with ice floes. Monet's impressions of the severe winter of 1879–80 inspired him to paint these pictures. On January 4, 1880, after an extraordinarily cold December, there was a great thaw that caused a rapid breakup of the ice and considerable damage in the area. Almost immediately, a new drop in the temperature halted the destruction and suspended the landscape in a partially frozen state. The ice floes, preserved in great chunks, were piled on the shore or appeared as floating masses upon the quiet surface of the river (Isaacson, *The Crisis of Impressionism*). Following this impressive event, Monet busied himself with the theme, finishing studies prepared at the scene in his studio and transferring them into larger formats. The Winterthur picture is probably related to another version of the same scene which is found today in the Louvre.

Just as Monet's summertime landscapes are all glowing sun and shimmering heat, here everything is numb with cold, and nature seems to have died beneath the winter light—yet the Impressionist's eye has caught color even in the ice.

AUGUSTE RODIN

b. Paris, 1840
d. Meudon, 1917

Portrait of Pope Benedict XV

1915
Bronze
26.5 cm. high (10³/₈ in.)

In September 1914, Giacomo della Chiesa (1854–1922) was elected Pope, assuming the name of Benedict XV. A group of Francophiles in the Vatican made an arrangement for Rodin to make a portrait bust of him. Benedict expected a portrait in the manner of the great Baroque artists, such as Hyacinthe Rigaud. It is therefore not surprising that he soon became alarmed at "the intense physical and psychological scrutiny to which Rodin was subjecting him." (Tancock, *The Sculpture of Auguste Rodin*.) To Rodin's annoyance the Pope did not have the patience to sit still, and the bust was never completed. When the artist wanted to study the Pope's profile, Benedict turned his head. He even became angry when Rodin asked to observe him from an elevated position. Nevertheless, despite these difficulties, Rodin was able to portray Benedict masterfully, with great plasticity of style in which light and shadow interplay eloquently. He captured both the spiritual and the intellectual expression of this ecclesiastical sovereign. During the First World War, the Pope displayed an exceptional concern for prisoners of war, protested against inhuman forms of war, and submitted a peace proposal which failed. His close involvement is reflected in Rodin's portrait. The expression of the eyes, which had seen so much misery, and the already slightly sunken cheeks are represented with particular intensity. With this portrait Rodin created one of his most mature works. Other casts of this sculpture are in Paris (Musée Rodin), Geneva (Musée d'Art et d'Histoire), Los Angeles (County Museum of Art), Philadelphia (Rodin Museum), Tokyo (National Museum of Western Art), and in the Vatican (Istituto per le Opere di Religione).

179

PIERRE AUGUSTE RENOIR

b. Limoges, 1841
d. Cagnes, 1919

La Grenouillère

1869
Oil on canvas
65 x 92 cm. (25⁷/₈ x 36³/₁₆ in.)
Acquired 1931

Pierre Auguste Renoir was Oskar Reinhart's favorite painter and the "Am Römerholz" collection owns twelve of his paintings, several from the 1860s and 1870s. *La Grenouillère* dates from 1869 and is a jewel of Impressionist painting. It shows an island in the Seine between Chatou and Bougival, one of the favorite outing places of Parisians at that time. The island boasted a restaurant called Père Fournaise, familiar from Renoir's *Luncheon of the Boating Party* (1881; Phillips Collection, Washington), a landing dock for boats, and a bathing establishment. La Grenouillère has passed into literature through two stories by de Maupassant, *La Femme de Paul* and *Yvette*.

Renoir painted on this island for the first time in 1868. The following year he stayed there with Monet, and the two artists, often working side by side, captured the relaxed, cheerful atmosphere of the place and the period in several paintings. Our picture shows the influence of Monet in the lightly applied but bold brushwork.

PIERRE AUGUSTE RENOIR

Portrait of Victor Chocquet

1876
Oil on canvas
46 x 36 cm. (18^1/$_8$ x 14^3/$_{16}$ in.)

Victor Chocquet (1821–91), an employee at the Paris Customs Administration, was a great admirer of the paintings of Delacroix. He was also one of the first collectors of Impressionist pictures. Although his financial means were limited, he put together a choice collection, which was dispersed after his death. Of course at that time, one could purchase such pictures relatively inexpensively. "One needed only a little taste," said Renoir in reference to Chocquet's collecting activity. The two became acquainted at the Impressionist exhibition in the Hôtel Drouot in 1875. Chocquet promptly commissioned the artist to paint a portrait of his wife posing in front of a painting by Delacroix. "I would like to have both of them together, my wife and Delacroix." (Vollard, *Auguste Renoir.*) This picture is currently in the Staatsgalerie, Stuttgart. The following year he himself was painted twice by Renoir. The second portrait is now in the Fogg Art Museum of Harvard University. Cézanne also created several portraits of Chocquet.

The Winterthur portrait shows a sensitive man sitting on a chair in front of a light green, flowered wallpaper. He has a narrow face, high forehead, and silken hair. It is a work which, though painted in oils, uses a soft feathery brushstroke that produces the effect of pastels.

183

PIERRE AUGUSTE RENOIR

Confidences

1878
Oil on canvas
61.5 x 50.5 cm. (24^1/$_4$ x 19^7/$_8$ in.)
Acquired 1923

This picture gives the impression of a snapshot; it captures an instant that Renoir invests with universal and timeless validity. The viewer surprises two young women in conversation, the intimate character of which is expressed by the arrangement of the figures. The subjects represented are Eva and Laurenzie, two of the artist's studio models. (Koella, *Sammlung Oskar Reinhart, Am Römerholz.*) The play of flecks of light, and especially the soft, loose, and merging colors lend this scene an exceptional enchantment. The space is reduced to a minimum and the young women become part of the background. In this painting, Rococo coloring is coupled with an impressionistic perception. The total effect has great charm and reminds one of the words of Renoir: "For me a picture must, above all, be something charming, lovely, and pleasing. Yes, something lovely. There are enough annoying things in life; it isn't necessary that we should bring still more into the world." (Photiadès, *Renoir.*) Renoir seldom achieved so much grace and freshness as in this picture.

185

PIERRE AUGUSTE RENOIR

The Sleeper

1897
Oil on canvas
82 x 66 cm. (32¼ x 26 in.)

Renoir was above all a painter of women. Throughout his career he glorified them in all possible poses and situations, dressed, half-dressed, or nude. In *The Sleeper*—this enchanting picture of a nude—Renoir has captured all the charm of the young woman. The voluptuousness and the delicate colors of her relaxed body seem to be heightened to express the very fullness of life and the utter pleasure of it. The eyes are closed, the lids drawn over them like soft veils, and the lips are slightly parted. One can almost see her breathing. (Jedlicka, "An den Rand geschrieben.")

Stylistically, the picture falls at the end of Renoir's so-called "mother-of-pearl period," which extended over almost the entire decade of the 1890s, and which connects the artist's classicist period—his Ingres period—to his late style. Sculptural fullness unites with Impressionist luminosity, and the soft, cool, pastel tones suggest the opalescence of iridescent seashells.

187

PAUL CEZANNE

b. Aix-en-Provence, 1839
d. Aix-en-Provence, 1906

Fruit Dish and Apples

Ca. 1877
Oil on canvas
55 x 74.5 cm. (21⁵/₈ x 29⁵/₁₆ in.)
Acquired 1921

Paul Cézanne, along with Toulouse-Lautrec and Van Gogh, was among the most prominent personalities of French Post-Impressionism. Cézanne was a great innovator who foreshadowed the moderns of the twentieth century. He broke away from the fluid, flickering treatment of color used by the Impressionists, introducing, to use his own words, "solidity and structure into the alignment of all things." (Rewald, *The History of Impressionism*.) Oskar Reinhart collected ten works, oils and watercolors, by this master.

This still life with fruit is from the same period as Cézanne's self-portrait in the Reinhart Collection (see page 191). It belongs to the beginning of his "Constructive period." At that time, Cézanne painted a series of still lifes: bowls and apples on a table in front of a patterned wallpaper. Paul Gauguin acquired the most important of these paintings, and it appeared in the center of the artists' group portrait by Maurice Denis, *Hommage à Cézanne* (Musée National d'Art Moderne, Paris). Cézanne chose to study the same table repeatedly, with its objects arranged only slightly differently from one version to the next. In his still lifes he preferred apples and oranges because of their sculptural, rounded forms, and also because they kept well, since he sometimes worked for months at a time on one picture. Furthermore, in the works of Cézanne and Courbet, apples are also interpreted erotically or at least refer to the abundance of life and fertility. (Schapiro, "The Apples of Cézanne.")

In the Winterthur still life the table is shown seen from above. The painting demonstrates how the introduction of geometry went hand in hand with the abstraction of the objective. Natural elements are reduced to simple, basic geometric forms and are inserted into the composition; solid permanence replaces the ephemeral. With this, the traditional concept of the still life—as it is interpreted, for example, by Chardin—changed as well; "Instead there came into being the *nature morte* in the true sense of the words." (Hüttinger, *Sammlung Emil G. Bührle*.)

189

PAUL CEZANNE

Self-Portrait

1879–82
Oil on canvas
33.5 x 24.5 cm. (13³/₁₆ x 9⁵/₈ in.)

Cézanne's frequent, analytical self-portraits remain unique in Mediterranean art. Usually such self-portraits are found among artists from northern Europe, for instance, Dürer, Rembrandt, Van Gogh, and Hodler.

The self-portrait we see here was painted around 1880. As with most self-portraits by Cézanne, it reduces the figure to head and shoulders, and concentrates on the expression of the face with its high forehead, slightly hooked nose, and sharply outlined, almond-shaped eyes which observe and contemplate the viewer. This painting once belonged to Degas. Incidentally, Oskar Reinhart had a marked preference for works that had previously been in the possession of artists or writers.

191

PAUL CEZANNE

Le Pilon du Roi

Ca. 1890–94
Oil on canvas
81.5 x 100.5 cm. (32$\frac{1}{16}$ x 39$\frac{9}{16}$ in.)
Acquired 1923

After about 1880, Cézanne became interested in the rocky prominence called the Pilon du Roi, which rises near Aix-en-Provence. He was staying at the time in Montbriand near "Bellevue," an estate that belonged to his brother-in-law. (Koella, *Sammlung Oskar Reinhart Am Römerholz.*)

The Winterthur painting, which recalls classical landscape compositions by Poussin, hints at a tendency toward geometric dissection, although not as markedly as in other contemporary works, such as *View of the Château Noir*, also in the Reinhart Collection. Here, Cézanne carried out the program which he had formulated: "to do Poussin over entirely from Nature." He found congruity between what he thought and what he saw. Thus he adhered to the topography of the landscape. The impression of nature is given classical strength through the strict formal structure and the controlled application of color, brushstroke by brushstroke. In the Winterthur picture, in contrast to related earlier versions, the trunk of the tree in the foreground has been cropped out of the picture, so that the branches appear suspended like a curtain. The structure of the picture already points toward abstract art.

Le Pilon du Roi comes from the collection of the Danish shipowner Hansen. When he wanted to sell his collection, the art dealers tried to depress prices. Reinhart's offers, on the other hand, were serious, and he was able to select what he wanted. In addition to the present picture, Reinhart purchased works by Corot, Delacroix, Daumier, and Renoir. The dealers and the Danish Government thereupon tried to cancel the sales in order to keep the collection in Denmark. However, the grateful shipowner remained firm and honored his commitment to Reinhart (Stettler, in Koella, *Sammlung Oskar Reinhart Am Römerholz.*)

PAUL CEZANNE

Mont Ste.-Victoire

Ca. 1904–06
Watercolor
47.2 x 62.6 cm. (18 9/16 x 24 5/8 in.)
Acquired 1923

Mont Ste.-Victoire, with its characteristic silhouette, was represented by Cézanne in a large series of oils, watercolors, and drawings. It emerged as an independent pictorial theme in his work in the 1880s, and he continued to paint the landscape up to his death. His statements to the French poet Joachim Gasquet testify to the painter's love for this mountain: "Look at this Mont Ste.-Victoire. What movement, what territorial thirst for sun and what melancholy at evening, when the heaviness [of night] sinks down upon it." (*Ueber die Kunst.*)

In 1901, Cézanne built himself a studio on the Chemin des Lauves, a few kilometers north of Aix; this watercolor was painted there. The artist has stylized the landscape, and captured the enduring, the immovable, and the lasting, freed from the climatic, seasonal, or daily changes which were so significant for the Impressionists. Depth of space is abandoned, and foreground and background begin to merge. Cézanne was concerned with watercolor technique throughout all periods of his career.

195

VINCENT VAN GOGH

b. Groot-Zundert, Holland, 1853
d. Auvers-sur-Oise, France, 1890

The Courtyard of the Asylum in Arles

1889
Oil on canvas
73 x 92 cm. (28³/₄ x 36¹/₄ in.)
Acquired 1923

Vincent van Gogh, one of the most tragic figures in nineteenth-century art, felt himself attracted to the abandoned and despised. As a result of a nervous breakdown in 1889, he spent a year in a hospital at Arles. While there, he painted numerous pictures, such as this view of the hospital courtyard, seen from the gallery of the first floor. But the view presented here shows more than the artist could have seen from any one vantage point, demonstrating the breadth of his creative imagination. The fact that the flower beds have been planted but that the trees are not yet in leaf tells us that the picture was painted in early spring. Goldfish can be seen in the central pool. At first sight, the whole scene seems pleasant and decorative; only on closer inspection do we see the depression and tragedy that this building represented for Van Gogh. For example, the patients are confined to the arcades and galleries and seem excluded from the springtime splendor of the garden. Similarly, the gnarled trees in the foreground appear to symbolize the physical and spiritual misery of the patients (Koella, *Sammlung Oskar Reinhart Am Römerholz*).

196

197

VINCENT VAN GOGH

Ward in the Asylum in Arles

1889
Oil on canvas
72 x 91 cm. (28³/₈ x 35⁷/₈ in.)
Acquired 1925

As in *The Courtyard of the Asylum in Arles* (see page 197), the interior view of the hospital, seen here, and painted somewhat later, is oppressive and enclosed. As Van Gogh described it: "A very long hall with rows of white-curtained beds along the walls. A few of the patients can be seen. The walls, and the ceiling with its heavy beams, are both white—a white with a tinge of lilac or green. Here and there is a window with a pink or light green curtain. The floor is of red tiles. At the back there is a door with a crucifix above it." (*Letters*.) It seems doubtful whether the third figure from the left is really a self-portrait, as has sometimes been suggested. Almost any one of these patients could have been Van Gogh, "so entirely capable was he of identifying his own fate with that of outsiders and that of outsiders with his own." (Schmidt, *Van Gogh*.)

199

ARISTIDE MAILLOL

b. Banyuls-sur-Mer, 1861
d. Banyuls-sur-Mer, 1944

The Mediterranean

1905
Limestone
116 cm. high ($45^{11}/_{16}$ in.)
Acquired 1931

The Mediterranean occupies a prominent position among the works of Maillol, who was a decisive force in modern art. Maillol described this sculpture to Oskar Reinhart as the finest of his life. In it, everything that moved him was realized. The development of the piece has a long history: it was prepared with drawings; sculptural models in terracotta followed (one of which is to be found in the Reinhart Collection); and then came a larger-than-life figure in plaster, which André Gide admired. Maillol created his first version in stone for the German collector Harry Graf Kessler. In 1931, it became the property of Oskar Reinhart. In addition to this, there are also well-known replicas in bronze and marble, now in Perpignan and the Jardin des Tuileries in Paris.

The statue has been called by several names. The present title was not given by the artist. He merely called her *Sitting Woman*. She neither embodies a definite idea, nor illustrates a poetic vision. A massive, heavy woman simply sits, constructed as a closed, tectonic form. Her quiet posture, in which she is wholly absorbed, acts as a "primitive, unchangeable gesture of powerful aliveness." (Hackelsberger, *Aristide Maillol: La Méditerranée*.)

Maillol, in his unmistakable individuality, rarely sought to create the likeness of a particular person. Instead, he concentrated on generalized, superindividual types that can be read both as objective shapes and as universal symbols. Thus he could disregard realistic proportions and say: "The further one detaches oneself from Nature, the closer one comes to being an artist."

HENRI DE TOULOUSE-LAUTREC

b. Albi, 1864
d. Malromé Castle, Gironde, 1901

The Clown Cha-U-Kao

1895
Oil on canvas
75 x 55 cm. (29^1/$_2$ x 21^5/$_8$ in.)
Acquired 1922

Henri de Toulouse-Lautrec came from one of the oldest families of the French nobility. Crippled in his youth, he moved to Paris in 1881 and became an artist, a chronicler of the life of Montmartre and the environs of Paris. He worked repeatedly at the Moulin Rouge, and it was in the foyer of that famous cabaret that Cha-U-Kao, the female clown, dancer, and acrobat, posed for him.

The scene is almost like a poster in its emphatic graphic style. This is no accident, for Toulouse-Lautrec had been producing posters since 1891, and was one of the first non-commercial artists to do so. The dancer is shown in the foreground in a provocative position, legs spread apart. The weight of her bulky body rests on one leg, and she has pushed her left hand into the pocket of her blue-black pantaloons. Her face, with its double chin and snub nose, is puffy and heavily made up; the lips are colored an intense raspberry red. Behind her to the left we recognize Gabrielle la Danseuse and, at the right, next to the small round woman, the writer Tristan Bernard. At the back, before a glass partition, some women and men are sitting at small tables. As in a snapshot, the artist has captured the atmosphere of the Moulin Rouge completely, but behind all the glitter and colorful costumes he gives us a glimpse into human tragedies and failures.

203

PABLO PICASSO

b. Malaga, Spain, 1881
d. Mougins, France, 1973

Portrait of Mateu Fernández de Soto

1901
Oil on canvas
61 x 46.5 cm. (24 x 18⁵/₁₆ in.)
Acquired 1935

The "Am Römerholz" collection is rounded out by a painting from Picasso's Blue Period and three of his drawings completed in 1919. The portrait of his friend, the artist Mateu Fernández de Soto, is a breathtaking piece of melancholy poetry. It was painted in 1901 at the beginning of the Blue Period, as the predominant blue tone of the work proclaims. The artist's facial expression as he fills his pipe is introspective; the figure is somewhat elongated, especially the slim, almost brittle-looking fingers. In the top right-hand corner, we see an earlier Picasso picture, *Le Mort*, of which two versions exist. Whether this is the one that is now in the Petit Palais in Paris or whether it is the one now in an American private collection cannot be discerned.

205

Bibliography

Literature on Oskar Reinhart and his Collections

Budry, Paul. "La Collection Reinhart et la peinture française," *Formes et couleurs* 2/3:1940.

Cooper, Douglas. *Great Private Collections*. Introd. by Kenneth Clark. New York: Macmillan, 1973.

Courthion, Pierre. "La Collection Oskar Reinhart," *L'Amour de l'art* 7:1926.

Gantner, Joseph. "Oskar Reinhart. Zum 80. Geburtstag am 11. Juni 1965," *National-Zeitung* (Basel), 6 June 1965.

George, Waldemar. "Collection Oskar Reinhart: Topographie d'une collection," *Formes* 26/27:1932.

Häsli, Richard. "Die Sammlung Oskar Reinhart," *Neue Zürcher Zeitung*, 9 March 1970.

Heise, Carl Georg. "Die Stiftung Oskar Reinhart in Winterthur," *Das Werk* 38:1951; reprinted in Heise, Carl Georg. *Der gegenwärtige Augenblick*. Berlin: Mann, 1960.

Holz, Hans Heinz. "Sein ist Farbe—Die Sammlung Oskar Reinhart," *National-Zeitung* (Basel), 15 March 1970.

Huggler, Max. "Die Privatsammlung Oskar Reinhart, *Schweizer Monatshefte* 35: 1955.

Huth, Arno. "A Swiss Collection of Masterpieces Exhibited at the Berne Museum," *The Studio* 119:1940.

Jedlicka, Gotthard. "An den Rand geschrieben. Divagationen über Bilder der Sammlung Oskar Reinhart," *Du* 16:1956.

_____. "Oskar Reinhart. 11. Juni 1885 bis 16. September 1965," *Neue Zürcher Zeitung*, 21 September 1965.

Keller, Heinz. *Die Stiftung Oskar Reinhart. Verzeichnis der Gemälde und Plastiken*. 2d ed., rev. Winterthur, 1971.

Koella, Rudolf. *Sammlung Oskar Reinhart Am Römerholz. Mit Beiträgen von Michael Stettler und Eduard Hüttinger*. Zurich: Orell Füssli Verlag, 1975.

_____. "Sammlung Oskar Reinhart Am Römerholz, Winter-thur," *Schweizerischer Kunstführer*, 1975.

Meier-Graefe, Julius. "Die Sammlung Oskar Reinhart," *Frankfurter Zeitung*, 29 April and 12 May 1932.

Meisterwerke europäischer Malerei des 15–19. Jahrhunderts aus der Sammlung Oskar Reinhart. 4 portfolios, Hans Zbinden, ed. Bern: Iris Verlag, 1940/41.

Scheffler, Karl. "Die Sammlung Oskar Reinhart in Winterthur," *Kunst und Künstler* 25:1926.

Schmidt, Georg. "Die Sammlung Oskar Reinhart. Zur Ausstellung in der Kunsthalle," *National-Zeitung* (Basel), 22 April and 3 May 1932.

Seiffert-Wattenberg, Richard. *Aus der Sammlung Oskar Reinhart*. Munich: Bruckmann, 1935.

Stähelin, Lisbeth. "Die Sammlung Oskar Reinhart 'Am Römerholz,'" *Winterthurer Jahrbuch*, 1970.

_____. *Sammlung Oskar Reinhart "Am Römerholz."* Winterthur: Swiss Confederation, 1970.

_____. "Sammlung Oskar Reinhart 'Am Römerholz,'" *Grosse Gemäldegalerien, herausgegeben von Erich Steingräber*. Munich: Hirmer, 1980.

Stettler, Michael. "Oskar Reinhart," *Rat der Alten, Begegnungen und Besuche*. 3d ed., rev. Bern, 1980.

Vignau-Wilberg, Peter. *Stiftung Oskar Reinhart Winterthur*. Vol. 2: *Deutsche und Österreichische Maler*. Zurich: Orell Füssli Verlag, 1979.

Vitali, Lamberto. "Le grandi collezioni. I: La raccolta Oskar Reinhart a Winterthur," *Emporium* 43:1937.

Zelger, Franz. "Stiftung Oskar Reinhart, Winterthur," *Schweizerischer Kunstführer*, 1974.

_____. *Stiftung Oskar Reinhart*. Vol. 1 *Schweizer Maler des 18. und 19. Jahrhunderts*. Zurich: Orell Füssli Verlag, 1977.

Literature Mentioned in the Text

Baudelaire, Charles. *Curiosités esthétiques*. Présentation par Julien Cain. *Miroirs d'art*. Paris: Hermann, 1968.

Böcklin, Angela. *Böcklin Memoiren. Tagebuchblätter von Böcklins Gattin Angela, mit dem gesamten brieflichen Nachlass*. Ed. Ferdinand Runkel. Berlin: Internationale Verlagsanstalt für Kunst und Literatur, 1910.

Börsch-Supan, Helmut, and Jähnig, Karl Wilhelm. *Caspar David Friedrich, Gemälde, Druckgraphik und bildmässige Zeichnungen*. Munich: Prestel Verlag, 1973.

Cézanne, Paul. *Ueber die Kunst. Gespräche mit Gasquet und Briefe*. Hamburg, Rowohlt, 1957.

Champfleury (Jules Fleury Husson). *Histoire de la caricature moderne*. Paris, 1871.

Constable, John. *Correspondence*. R. B. Beckett, ed. Suffolk: Records Society, 1966.

Courbet und Deutschland. Exhibition catalogue. Kunsthalle, Hamburg, 1978; Galerie im Städelschen Kunstinstitut, Frankfurt, 1979.

Diderot, Denis. *Oeuvres esthétiques*. Paris: Garnier, 1968.

Fleischmann, Benno. *Honoré Daumier*. Vienna: Otto Lorenz, 1938.

Frère, Henri. *Conversations de Maillol*. Geneva: P. Cailler, 1956.

Guillaume, Germaine. "Avant l'impressionisme en Suisse, Alexandre Calame." *Amour de l'art*, Oct./Nov. 1939.

Van Gogh, Vincent. *The Complete Letters of Vincent van Gogh*. Johanna Bonger and E. de Dood, eds. London: Thames and Hudson, 1958.

Hackelsberger, Berthold. *Aristide Maillol: La Méditerranée. Werkmonographien zur bildenden Kunst*, no. 56. Stuttgart: Philipp Reclam jun., 1960.

Hüttinger, Eduard. *Sammlung Emil G. Bührle*. Zürich: Kunsthaus Zurich, 1958.

————. *Degas*. Cologne: Uffici, 1960.

Ingres, Jean Auguste Dominique. *Du dessin. Ingres, raconté par lui-même et par ses amis*. Geneva: P. Cailler, 1947.

Isaacson, Joel. *The Crisis of Impressionism 1878–1882*. Ann Arbor: University of Michigan Museum of Art, 1980.

Koepplin, Dieter. *Cranachs Ehebildnis des Johannes Cuspinian*. Basel: Universität Basel, 1974.

Lankheit, Klaus. *Revolution und Restauration*. Baden-Baden: Holle, 1965.

Leslie, Charles Robert. *Memoirs of the Life of John Constable*. 2d ed. Oxford: Phaidon, 1980.

Maupassant, Guy de. "La Vie d'un paysagiste," *Oeuvres posthumes*. Paris: Louis Conrad, 1910.

Meier-Graefe, Julius. *Entwicklungsgeschichte der modernen Kunst*. Stuttgart: J. Hoffmann, 1904.

Moreau-Nélaton, Etienne. *Corot, raconté par lui-même*. Paris: Laurens, 1924.

Photiadès, Vassily. *Renoir: Nus, collection rythmes et couleurs*. Lausanne: International Art Books, 1960.

Rewald, John. *The History of Impressionism*. New York: Museum of Modern Art, 1973.

Schapiro, Meyer. "The Apples of Cézanne: An Essay on the Meaning of Still Life," *Modern Art: 19th and 20th Centuries*. New York: Braziller, 1978.

Schmidt, Georg. *Van Gogh*. Bern: Scherz, 1947.

Tancock, John L. *The Sculpture of Auguste Rodin*. Philadelphia: David R. Godine, 1976.

Thoma, Hans. *Im Herbst des Lebens. Gesammelte Erinnerungsblätter*. Munich: Süddeutsche Monatshefte, 1909.

————. *Im Winter des Lebens. Aus acht Jahrzehnten gesammelte Erinnerungen*. Jena: Eugen Diederichs, 1919.

Venturi, Lionello. *Impressionists and Symbolists*. New York: Scribner's, 1950.

Vollard, Ambroise. *Auguste Renoir*. Paris: Editions G. Crès, 1920.

Voss, Hermann. "Die Flucht nach Aegypten," *Saggi e memorie di storia dell'arte* 1/1957.

Index of Artists